Eustace Clare Grenville Murray

The Oyster; where, how and when to find, breed, cook and eat it

Eustace Clare Grenville Murray

The Oyster; where, how and when to find, breed, cook and eat it

ISBN/EAN: 9783744789745

Printed in Europe, USA, Canada, Australia, Japan

Cover: Foto ©Andreas Hilbeck / pixelio.de

More available books at **www.hansebooks.com**

WHERE, HOW, AND WHEN

to

FIND, BREED, COOK,

and

EAT IT.

LONDON:

TRÜBNER & CO., 60, PATERNOSTER ROW.

MDCCCLXI.

CONTENTS.

CHAPTER I.

THE OYSTER IN SEASON.

CHAPTER II.

ANCIENT HISTORY OF THE OYSTER.

CHAPTER III.

MODERN HISTORY OF THE OYSTER.

CHAPTER IV.

THE OYSTER AT HOME.

CHAPTER V.

THE OYSTER IN ITS NEW SETTLEMENT.

CHAPTER VI.

THE OYSTER ON ITS TRAVELS.

CHAPTER VII.

THE OYSTER AT ITS JOURNEY'S END.

CHAPTER VIII.

THE OYSTER AND THE DOCTOR.

CHAPTER IX.

THE OYSTER ABROAD.

CHAPTER X.

"THE TREASURE OF AN OYSTER."

THE OYSTER.

CHAPTER I.

The R. canon correct; Alimentary Qualities of the Oyster;
Profitable Investment; Billingsgate, and London Con-
sumption; English Oyster-beds; Jersey Oysters; French
Oyster-beds on the Coast of Brittany.

F THE MILLIONS who live to eat
and eat to live in this wide
world of ours, how few are
there who do not, at proper
times and seasons, enjoy a
good oyster. It may not
be an ungrateful task,
therefore, if I endeavour
to inform them what spe-
cies of animal the little
succulent shell - fish is,
that affords to man so
much gastronomical en-
joyment—how born and
bred and nurtured; when,
and where; and, lastly, how best it may be eaten,
whether in its living and natural state, or having

B

undergone the ordeal of cooking by the skill of a superior artist.

I have oftentimes been told that it is a mere question of fastidiousness, or fashion, that oysters should be served for human food only at a certain fixed period of the year—those months possessing the letter *r* being proverbially the only months when the oyster is fit for human food. Why not, such reasoners have said, eat oysters all the year round? Life is short. Why not obtain the first of gastronomical enjoyments every month of the year and every day of the month? I can in no manner go with these opinions, either from my practical knowledge of the oyster, or from any just reasoning.

I am aware that there are many good men and true, and others calling themselves, somewhat erroneously, sportsmen, beyond the white cliffs of Britain, who would eat an oyster on the hottest day of June and July as they would a partridge, a pheasant, or a salmon at any season of the year. Sufficient the names oyster, partridge, pheasant—all gastronomical delights—all to be eaten, and by them eaten whensoever and wheresoever served, what matters it? I am also aware that in our good City of London, in the hottest and earliest days of August,* oysters are gulped down by

---

* The common Colchester and Faversham oysters are brought to market on the 5th of August. They are called *Common oysters*, and are picked up on the French coast, and then transferred to those beds; the Milton, or, as they are commonly called, the *melting Natives*, the true Rutupians, do not come in till the beginning of October, continue in season till the 12th of May, and approach the meridian of their perfection about Christmas. The denizens from France are not

the thousand: it is, nevertheless, an error—a revolting, unhealthy, unclean error—which ought to be denied, both at home and abroad, by the strong hand of the law.

I, for my part, utterly and entirely ignore fish or fowl of the game species, as fit for human food during the seasons of breeding; and although an oyster may be eatable in August, if the month be hot it is rarely fresh; and what is more disgusting or more likely to be injurious to man than a stale oyster? That which I have said, however, on the oyster in this little book which I offer to the million—for the million are interested in the subject—will, I hope, induce those who have hitherto broken through a rule strictly adhered to by all gastronomes, to abstain in future; and those who have hitherto enjoyed oyster-eating, fearlessly to eat on and secure the first and foremost of all gastronomical indulgences provided for man—only in due season.

On the 25th of July, says Brand, the antiquary, being St. James the Apostle's Day, the priests of old were wont to bless apples; and a popular belief too, in 1588, though generally ignored in the more enlightened days in which we live, was, that whoever ate oysters on that day would not be without money for the remainder of the year. This is very probable, for without they were selected with great care, disease and even death might follow. This conjunction of apples and oysters on St. James's Day may have suggested Bianca's remark

to be compared to British *Native* oysters, which are so called because they are born, bred, and fed in this country. These do not come to perfection till they are four years old.

in the "Taming of the Shrew," when comparing the resemblance of the old Pedant to that of Vincentio, which she remarks was as complete as that of an oyster to an apple.

One must, therefore, take care not to eat oysters during the months of June and July, because they are unwholesome on account of the spawning-time; and also be careful in their selection in August. There are instances when persons, after having eaten oysters during these months, have become ill, and have even died. Last summer, at Ostend, thirty persons were taken ill in consequence of having eaten oysters in the month of July. They are, during these months, very thin, and without taste; in the month of September they become again fat and eatable, which may be accounted for by the fact of their being self-generated. The strength of the poor oysters is entirely spent in fattening themselves, in order the more to tickle the palate of the epicure in the proper season.

Now let us proceed to open the oyster.

The Oyster! The mere writing of the word creates sensations of succulence—gastronomical pleasures, nutritive food, easy digestion, palatable indulgence—then go sleep in peace!

Lobster salads, beef and veal, truffles and chestnuts, all good in their way, are, nevertheless, attended with evil consequences to the human frame.

But oysters—ye pleasant companions of the midnight hours, or the mid-day feast; is there a man, woman, or child in all Europe—ay, or in Asia, Africa, or America —who does not owe you a debt of gratitude which they repay to the full by the enjoyment of your society *tête-à tête?* You are eaten raw and alive, cooked and scolloped, in sauce and without sauce. True, true, oh oyster! thou art the best beloved of the loved !.

The oyster, when eaten moderately, is, without contradiction, a wholesome food, and one of the greatest delicacies in the world. It contains much nutritive substance, which is very digestive, and produces a peculiar charm and an inexplicable pleasure. After having eaten oysters we feel joyous, light, and agreeable— yes, one might say, fabulously well. He who has eaten for the first time oysters is best enabled to judge of this; for, soon after having eaten them, he will experience a sensation he never felt before, and never had an idea of. This sensation scarcely remains with people who eat oysters every day; it is more practically felt when oysters are eaten for breakfast or before dinner, although they are also very wholesome in the evening, when taken moderately. Gourmets and epicures eat the oyster in its natural state, except that the beard is taken away. In England it is eaten with pepper, in Holland with vinegar, in Germany frequently with lemon-juice; but I am of the opinion, and am convinced, that when taken with the liquor they still contain, they are more digestible and more tasty. The opinion that this fluid is salt water, is an error; it is the white blood of the oyster itself, which it emits when injured in having its upper shell broken off. If it were sea-water, it would have a disagreeable bitter taste, and cause sickness; but as this does not take place, but on the contrary gives a fine taste to the oyster, the error is evident. The error appears to arise from the fact that unconscientious oyster dealers wash the oysters with salt and water in order to give them a better appearance, as they say.

"The oyster," says a writer in No. 824 of the "Family Herald"—that most agreeable of all window-seat books—"is a species of food combining the most precious alimentary qualities. Its meat is soft, firm, and delicate. It has sufficient flavour to please the taste, but not enough to excite to surfeit. Through a quality peculiar to itself, it favours the intestinal and gastric absorption, mixing easily with other food; and, assimilating with the juices of the stomach, it aids and favours the digestive functions. There is no other alimentary substance, not even excepting bread, which does not produce indigestion under certain given circumstances, but oysters never. This is a homage due to them. They may be eaten to-day, to-morrow, for ever, in profusion; indigestion is not to be feared, and we may be certain that no doctor was ever called in through their fault. Of course we except cooked oysters. Besides their valuable digestive qualities, oysters supply a recipe not to be despised in the liquor they contain. It is produced by the sea-water they have swallowed, but which, having been digested, has lost the peculiar bitterness of salt water. This oyster-water is limpid, and slightly saline in taste. Far from being purgative, like sea-water, it promotes digestion. It keeps the oysters themselves fresh, prolongs their life for some time until it is destroyed in our stomachs, or until the oyster has been transformed into a portion of ourselves."

The degree of importance which different persons

attach to matters connected with the world in which
we live, depends, of course, in a great measure, on the
manner in which they view them.

One person considers a loving wife, and four hundred a year, wealth and happiness; another would be
miserable without four thousand, and could dispense
with the wife. Some consider a post with five thousand
a year a tolerable means of existence ; others a commis-
sionership with twelve hundred. Some seek a good
consulship; others, till they have travelled from St.
Petersburg and back in a telega, or sledge, half a dozen
times during mid-winter, use the interest, which in
other days would have secured a snug governorship,
even in the Island of Barataria, to obtain a queen's
messenger's place. At least so it used to be. Whether
competitive examinations will lead to our having the
right man in the right place, the round pegs in round
holes, and the square pegs in square ones, still remains
to be seen. And so is it with most things in life,
whether personal or gastronomical. Different men are
of different opinions ; some like apples, and some like—
onions ; but I have scarcely ever yet met with the man
who has refused a thoroughly good oyster.

There is not a man, however unobservant, but knows
that oysters are a great source of profit to some of that
multitude which rises every morning without knowing
exactly how, when, and where it shall dine. Billingsgate in the oyster season is a sight and a caution. Boats
coming in loaded; porters struggling with baskets and
sacks; early loungers looking on—it is so pleasant to
see other people work—buyers and cheapeners, the fish

salesman in his rostrum, the wealthy purchaser who can lay out his hundreds and buy his thousands—all to be met with, together with that noise and bustle, and, far beyond it, all that incredible earnestness which always distinguishes an English market.

Oysters, says Dryasdust, in his very useful commercial work—in which, however, he makes alarming misstatements—oysters are consumed in London in incredible quantities, "and notwithstanding their high price, are largely eaten by the middle and lower classes!"

Thanking Dryasdust for his information, and being one of the great middle class ourselves, we can safely assert that oysters are *not* high in price. Fancy being able to purchase twelve succulent dainties for one sixpence at Ling's or Quin's, at Proctor's or Pim's, or any other celebrated shell-fish shop! Twelve "lumps of delight," as the Mussulman—not mussel man—calls his sweetmeats! and then fancy Dryasdust saying that they are high in price! Oh shame, where is thy blush!

A farm of four acres, if well handled, may give occupation, and even bring pecuniary gain, to the possessor. A garden, for those who thoroughly understand and enjoy it, may secure untold pleasures, and perhaps help to pay the rent of the cottage. But an "oyster-bed" is a pleasure—an *el dorado*—a mine of wealth, in fact, which fills the owners' pockets with gold, and affords to the million untold gastronomical enjoyment and healthy food. On the money part of the question, the Scientific and Useful column, of Number 825 of the "Family Herald" furnishes the following information : "A very interesting report has been recently made to the French Government on the results of experiments made for the improvement of oyster-beds. The locality chosen was the bay of St. Brieux, on the coast of Brittany. Between March and May, 1859, about 3,000,000 oysters, taken from different parts of the sea, were distributed in ten longitudinal beds in the above bay. The bottom was previously covered with old oyster shells and boughs of trees arranged like fascines. To these the young oysters attach themselves, and so fruitful are the results that one of the fascines was found at the end of six months to have no less than 20,000 young oysters on it. The report further states that 12,000 hectares may be brought into full bearing in three years at an annual expense not exceeding 10,000 francs."

M. Laviciare, Commissary of the Maritime Inscription, in his 1860 report to M. Coste, of the success of these operations in the Bay of St. Brieux, states that " a recent examination has fully and satisfactorily proved the advantageous results obtained on the five banks which have been laid down, and which have exceeded the most sanguine expectations. Three fascines, which were taken up indiscriminately from one of the banks formed in June, 1859, contained about 20,000 oysters each, of from one inch to two inches in diameter. The total expense for forming the above bank was 221f.; and if the 300 fascines laid down on it be multiplied by 20,000, 600,000 oysters will be obtained, which, if sold at 20f. a thousand, will produce 120,000f. If, however, the number of oysters on each fascine were to be reckoned at only 10,000, the sum of 60,000f. would be received, which, for an expenditure of only 221f. would give

a larger profit than any other known branch of in-
dustry."

But the breeding and fattening of the London oyster
has long been a lucrative branch of trade, of which
Cockaine may well be proud. It is carried on "con-
tagious" to London, as Mrs. Malaprop would say—
principally in Essex and Kent. The rivers Crouch,
Blackwater, and Colne are the chief breeding places
in the former, and the channel of the Swale and the
Medway in the latter. These are contiguous to Milton;
hence Dibdin's song, and hence also the corruption of
"melting hoysters;" melting they are too. The corruption is classical, so let it stand.

Exclusive of oysters bred in Essex and Kent, vast
numbers are brought from Jersey, Poole, and other places
along the coast, and are fattened in beds. The export
of oysters from Jersey alone is very considerable, having amounted on an average of the four years ending
with 1832* to 208,032 bushels a year. The Jersey
fishing then employed, during the season, about 1500
men, 1000 women and children, and 250 boats. Think
of this, ye oyster-eaters! Think that ye are doing—such
is the wise ordination of an overruling Providence—some
good when you are swallowing your ante-prandial
oyster, and are giving employment to some portion of
those 3000 people who work for you at Jersey, besides
helping to feed the cold-fingered fishmonger, who, with
blue apron and skilful knife, tempts you to " Hanother
dazzen, sir ?"

* The exportation has by this time nearly doubled, but these
are the latest statistics we can arrive at.

Of the quantity of oysters consumed in London we cannot give even an approximate guess. It must amount to millions of bushels. Fancy, if you can, also, that curiously courteous exchange which goes on every Christmas between our oyster-eating country cousins and our turkey and goose-loving Londoners. To the man

> "Who hath been long in city pent,
> 'Tis very sweet to gaze upon the fair
> And open brow of heaven ;—to breathe a prayer
> Full in the face of the blue firmament"—

sings John Keats. Oh, if he had been but an oyster-eater, that article from the "Quarterly," savage and slaughterly, would not have killed him; but it is also very sweet to gaze upon a turkey, a leash of birds, a brace of pheasants, and, as Mrs. Tibbetts hath it, "a real country hare." Such a present is promptly repaid by a fine cod packed in ice, and two barrels of oysters. How sweet are these when eaten at a country home, and opened by yourselves, the barrel being paraded on the table with its top knocked out, and with the whitest of napkins round it, as we shall presently have occasion to show. How sweet it is, too, to open some of the dear natives for your pretty cousin, and to see her open her sweet little mouth about as wide as Lesbia's sparrow did for his lump of—not sugar, it was not then invented—but lump of honey! How sweet it is, after the young lady has swallowed her half dozen, to help yourself! The oyster never tastes sweeter than when thus operated on by yourself, so that you do not "job" the knife into your hand! True labour has a

dignity about it. The only time when I, who have
seen most people, from Tom Thumb to the Benicia Boy,
from Madame Doche to the Empress Eugenie, and from
manly, sea-going Prince Alfred to the Staleybridge
Infant and Jemmy Shaw's "Spider"—the only time, I
say, that I have ever seen a nobleman look like a nobleman, was when a noble duke, a peer not only of
England and Scotland, but of *la belle France* also, owned
that he could do two things better than most people,
and that was, open oysters and polish his own boots.
I, like Othello, when he upbraided Iago for the last
time, "looked down to his feet," but found that it
was no fable.

So important is our illustrious bivalve as an article
of trade, that it is protected by law. It is said that the
only two things that George the Fourth ever did—the
great Georgius, whom Mr. Thackeray envies and satirises
—were to invent a shoe-buckle and an exquisite hair-dye.,
The brains of the black Brunswicker could do no more.
But there is one act also—an Act of Parliament*—which
was passed in his reign, for which he is to be thanked.
The man who was at once the Lucullus and Apicius of
his times must have had some hand in the framing of
that Act.

* See page 25.

CHAPTER II.

ANCIENT HISTORY OF THE OYSTER.

The Ancients; Oysters a Greek and Roman Luxury; Sergius
Orata and the Oyster-beds of Baia; Immense Consump-
tion at Rome; Failure of the Circean and Lucrinian
Oyster-beds under Domitian, and Introduction of Rutupians
from Britain; Agricola, Constantine, and Helena; Athenian
Oysters and Aristides.

HORACE, Martial, and Juvenal, Cicero and Seneca,
Pliny, Ætius, and the old Greek doctor Oribasius,
whom Julian the Apostate delighted to honour, and
other men of taste amongst the ancients, have enlarged
upon the various qualities of the oyster; and was it
not to Sergius Orata that we owe our present oyster-
beds; for he it was who introduced layers or stews for
oysters at Baia, the Brighton of ancient Rome, as we
have them at present. That was in the days when
luxury was rampant, and when men of great wealth, like
Licinius Crassus, the leviathan slave merchant, rose to
the highest honours; for this dealer in human flesh
in the boasted land of liberty, served the office of consul
along with Pompey the Great, and on one occasion required no less than 10,000 tables to accommodate all
his guests. How many barrels of oysters were eaten at
that celebrated dinner, the "Ephemerides"—as Plutarch
calls "The Times" and "Morning Post" of that day—
have omitted to state; but as oysters then took the

place that turtle-soup now does at our great City feeds, imagination may busy itself if it likes with the calculation. All we know is, that oysters then fetched very long prices at Rome, as the author of the " Tabella Cibaria" has not failed to tell us ; and then, as now, the high price of any luxury of the table was sure to make a liberal supply of it necessary, when a man like Crassus entertained half the city as his guests, to rivet his popularity.

But the Romans had a weakness for the " breedy creatures," as our dear old friend Christopher North calls them in his inimitable "Noctes." In the time of Nero, some sixty years later, the consumption of oysters in the " Imperial City" was nearly as great as it now is in the " World's Metropolis;" and there is a statement, which I recollect to have read somewhere, that during the reign of Domitian, the last of the twelve Cæsars, a greater number of millions of bushels were annually consumed at Rome than I should care to swear to. These oysters, however, were but Mediterranean produce—the small fry of Circe, and the smaller Lucrinians; and this unreasonable demand upon them quite exhausted the beds in that great fly-catcher's reign ; and it was not till under the wise administration of Agricola in Britain, when the Romans got their far-famed Rutupians from the shores of Kent, from Richborough and the Reculvers —the *Rutupi Portus* of the " Itinerary," of which the latter, the *Regulbium,* near Whitstable, in the mouth of the Thames, was the northern boundary—that Juvenal praised them as he does ; and he was right : for in the whole world there are no oysters like them ; and of all the "breedy creatures" that glide, or have ever glided down the throats of the human race, our "Natives" are probably the most delectable. Can we wonder, then, when Macrobius tells us that the Roman pontiffs in the fourth century never failed to have these Rutupians at table, particularly, feeling sure that Constantine the Great, and his mother, the pious Helena, must have carried their British tastes with them to Rome at that period.

The Greeks have not said much in praise of oysters; but then they knew nothing of Britain beyond its name, and looked upon it very much in the same light as we now regard the regions of the Esquimaux; and as to the little dabs of watery pulps found in the Mediterranean, what are they but oysters in name? Indeed, the best use the Athenians could make of them was to use their shells to ostracise any good citizen who, like Aristides, was too virtuous for a "Greek." However, on the plea that oysters are oysters, we presume—for it could not be on account of their flavour—"oysters," says the author of the "Tabella Cibaria," "were held in great esteem by the Athenians." No doubt when Constantine moved the seat of the Empire from Rome to Constantinople, he did not forget to have his Rutupians regularly forwarded; so, perhaps, after all it was our "Natives," which thus found their way into Greece, that they delighted in; and if so, the good taste of the Athenians need not be called into question; but, as in literature and the arts, in oyster-eating too, it deserves to be held up to commendation.

CHAPTER III.

MODERN HISTORY OF THE OYSTER.

Fall of the Rutupian Supremacy ; Louis IV. and William of Normandy ; Conquest of England, and Revival of Oyster-eating
in England ; The Oyster under Legal Protection ; American
Oysters.

WITH the fall of the Empire came also the fall of the
Rutupian supremacy ; and even the Roman Bri-
tons, driven into Brittany and the mountains of Wales
by their truculent Saxon persecutors, had to forego
these luxuries of the table, unless, perhaps, Prince
Arthur and his knights may now and then have opened
a bushel when they were seated over their wine in that
free and easy circle, which has become so celebrated as
to have formed a literature of its own.   From the fourth
century, to which Macrobius brought us, to the reign of
Louis IV. of France, the history of the oyster is a blank ;
but that king revived the taste for our favourite, and
during his captivity in Normandy brought it again into
request with his conqueror, Duke William ; so, when
the Normans invaded England under William the Conqueror—the descendant of that Duke William, little
more than a century later—they were not long in find-
ing out how much Kentish and Essex oysters were
preferable to those of France.

Since then the Oyster has held its own against all

comers, as one of the most welcome accessories to the table of rich and poor, and has been protected in his rights and immunities by various Acts of Parliament. "In the month of May oysters cast their spawn," says an old writer in the " Transactions of the Royal Society," "which the dredgers call spat, and this spawn cleaves to stones, old oyster-shells, pieces of wood, and other substances at the bottom of the sea, which is called cultch. During that month, by the law of the Admiralty Court, the dredgers have liberty to take every kind of oyster, whatsoever be its size. When they have taken them they gently raise with a knife the small brood from the cultch, and then they throw the cultch in again, to preserve the ground for the future, unless they are so newly spat, that they cannot be safely severed from the cultch, in which case they are permitted to take the stone or shell, which the spat is upon, one shell having often twenty spats. After the month of May, it is felony to carry away the cultch, and punishable to take any other oysters except those of the size of a half-crown piece, or such as when the two shells are shut will admit of a shilling to rattle between them." These brood and other oysters are carried to creeks of the sea, and thrown into the channel, which are called their beds or layers, where they grow and fatten, and in two or three years oysters of the smallest brood reach the standard size.

The property in oyster beds is defined by the 7 & 8 George IV., c. 29, s. 36, which makes it larceny for any person to steal any oyster or oyster brood from any oyster bed belonging to another person, if such bed is

sufficiently marked out and known as such; and even
the attempt to take either oysters or oyster brood from
such an oyster bed, though none be actually disturbed,
is a misdemeanor, punishable by fine or imprisonment,
or both, though nothing is to prevent the fishing for
floating fish within the limits of any oyster fishery.

The Admiralty Court also imposes great penalties
upon those who do not destroy a fish, which they call
Fivefingers (the crossfish, or common starfish of our
coasts), because it is supposed that that fish gets into the
oysters when they gape, and sucks them out. That it
is injurious to oyster beds may be true; for its food, in
part, consists of mollusks. It does not, however, walk
into the oyster bodily, as the Admiralty Court suggests,
but rather appears to overpower its prey by applying
some poisonous secretion, and pouting out the lobes of
the stomach, so as to convert them into a kind of pro-
boscis, and thus suck the mollusks from their shells.

The reason of the penalty for destroying the cultch is
that the ouse then will increase, and mussels and cockles
will breed there and destroy the oysters, because they
have no convenience for depositing their spat. Hence,
mud and sea-weeds are extremely injurious to the
" breedy creatures' " propagation and increase; for no
less than starfish, cockles, and mussels, other enemies
amongst shellfish and crustaceous animals, particularly
crabs and scollops, eagerly devour the oyster, when they
can capture it.

In America, where the quality of the native oyster,
though little inferior to the larger species of Britain, is
greatly over-rated, the legislature is now called upon to

make a similar provision for its protection against its greatest enemy, man. " It has been estimated," says a correspondent in No. 769 of the "Family Herald," "that the State of Virginia possesses an area of about 1,680,000 acres of oyster beds, containing about 784,000,000 bushels of oysters. It is also stated that the mother oyster spawns annually at least 3,000,000 ; yet, notwithstanding this enormous productive power, and the vast extent of oyster beds, there is danger of the oyster being exterminated unless measures are adopted to prevent fishermen from taking them at improper seasons of the year. It is therefore proposed to have either a flotilla of four steamboats employed to protect the oyster beds from piratical intruders, or to farm out the oyster beds to private contractors to do with them as they please."

CHAPTER IV.

THE OYSTER AT HOME:

Its Nature, Colour, and Structure; Natural Food; Perception
of the changes of Light; Uses of the Cilia; Fecundity and
Means of Propagation; Age; Fossil Oysters in Berkshire
and in the Pacific; Power of Locomotion.

THE Oyster belongs to those Mollusks which are
headless, having their gills in the form of membranous plates, and are named *Lamellibranchiata*, from
the Latin word *Lamella*, a plate; or *Conchæ*, the Latin
name for the whole family of oyster, scollop, cockle,
mussel, and other well-known bivalves. Properly
speaking, only six kinds are fit to take part in the
gastromal treat, to say nothing of the sanitary advan-
tages the family are good enough to provide for the
world at large. These six peculiar and most agreeable
aristocrats all belong to the family of the common
oyster, *Ostrea edulis*, by far the most important tribe,
and in fact, that in behalf of whose meritorious qualities
I have more particularly taken up my pen.

The oyster bears different names in accordance to the
localities in which it is found, whether on rocky ground,
mud, or sand, and has different colours in different
places. In Spain, oysters are found of a red and russet
colour; in Illyria they are brown, but the fish is black,
and in the Red Sea, of the colours of the rainbow. The
green oyster, the Parisian delicacy, is brought from

Brittany; but the same flavour and colour can be produced by putting oysters into pits where the water is about three feet deep in the salt marshes, and where the sun has great power. In these they become green in three or four days; for these colours are derived from the elementary substance on which they feed; not, however, that it produces any peculiar difference as to flavour. I may, however, as well decide at once that the green oyster is, to my taste, the oyster *par excellence*, in which decision I shall doubtless be borne out by most *gourmets* whose knowledge extends to a choice of the good things of this life.

I know, in this, some of my friends north of the Tweed may differ, and, if still living, amongst them I should have had to include Professor Wilson, so long the very life and soul of oyster-suppers and whisky-toddy. But nobody can judge of the true flavour of an oyster without well *masticating* his delicious food; and, by his own showing, both he and the "Shepherd" bolted their "Pandores." These same "Pandores," by the way, are large fat oysters, much relished in modern Athens, which are said to owe their superior excellence to the brackish contents of the pans of the adjacent salt-works of Prestonpans flowing out upon the beds. Taken away young and transferred to the Ostend beds, these Pandores furnish the very best oysters to be met with on the Continent, surpassing even the far-famed ones of Flensburg, in Holstein. Had "Christopher North" tickled the fish first to death with his incisors before he swallowed it, I might have submitted my judgment to his; but how can a man who bolted

his food be quoted as an authority in matters of taste?
At best, his must have been but an after-taste, a mere
bilious reminder of what the repast had been, in which
the whisky played as prominent a part as the "breedy
creatures" themselves.

But let us return. The lower shell (*) of the oyster
is concave, the upper flat. These shells are opened and
closed by the medium of a strong muscle acting upon

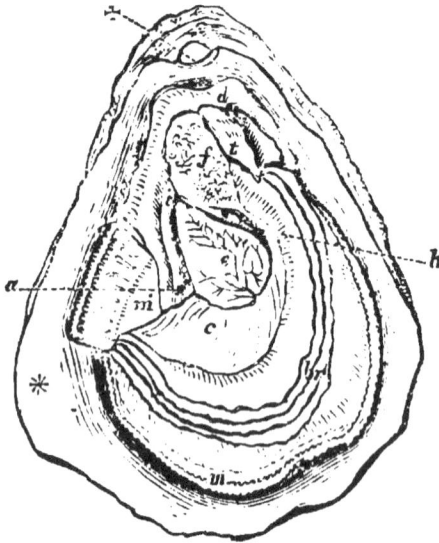

a hinge (†), far more complete in its structure than ever
locksmith could produce, even at the forthcoming Exhi-
bition of all Nations.

On the outside of the shell, when placed in a dark
place, we may often observe a shining matter of blueish
light, like a flame of brimstone, which sticks to the
fingers when touched, and continues shining and giving
light for a considerable time, though without any sensible heat. This light is produced by three varieties of

minute animalcules, most interesting when examined under the microscope.

The oyster possesses an organ of respiration similar to that of a fish—branchiæ or gills, in fact (*br*), which are fringed by a mantle or beard divided into two lobes (*m*), filled up by small membranous fibres which terminate in the mouth (*b*), in the form of rays, serving the animal also with power to catch and eat. Unlike other shelled mussels the oyster has no feet; thus it is unable to make any other voluntary movement, save that of opening and closing its shell, as already named, in order to receive its food, which consists principally of small microscopical spores and young shoots of marine plants, made soft and thin by the action of the waves; whence arise the green beards or mantles. With some difficulty I have been enabled to separate a small portion of this vegetation from the mantle of an oyster, and having placed it under a strong microscope, discovered sea weed, of precisely the same species as that in which oysters are packed. They also feed on an infusion of sea worms called oyster animalcules. These are very accurately described in the "Journal des Savans," by M. Auzout. Some are irridescent, but others are not, and good specimens of all may be secured immediately the oyster has been taken from the sea.

By means of the beard or mantle described (*m*), the oyster secures his food, bringing it gradually, by means of little hooks bent inwards, to its mouth (*b*), wherein it is crushed and slowly consumed.

The stomach (*i*) is situated near the mouth, and all the organs are very simple. The mantle (*m* and *m'*) above-named replaces the lungs. The liver (f) is small; the gall, comparatively speaking, large; the larger blood vessels little rarefied. The heart (h) consists of two cameras at a tolerable distance from one another, resembling small round bladders. The pulse beats rather slowly (caused by, perhaps, the want of food and sea water). From the stomach the rectum (a) leads directly to the anus. How digestion is effected in this short and simple way, I can scarce venture to assert. But it is a fact well known, that, after the spawning season, the oyster becomes thin, but a very short time enables it to recover its fat and succulence.

On examining the oyster the mantle (m), divided into two lobes (m and m'), the edges of which are fringed, will be perceived filling the greater part of the shell; also four membranous leaves crossed with stripes, which at their hinder extremities have as many capillary tubes. These leaves, or veins, unequally divided around the edges of the body perform the functions of the lungs, and separate from the water the necessary air for the maintenance of the animal.

The mouth (b) is a kind of trunk, or long aperture surrounded by four lips nearly resembling those of a gill, but far shorter.

Behind the muscles is to be seen a large fleshy white and cylindrical substance moving on a central muscle, and containing the stomach and intestines (i). This part resembles the trunk of other conchæ, but it has no power of opening or contracting. The canal of the intestines is situated on the top of the muscle (a).

The oyster has circular vessels, on the bottom of which

n deep muscular cavities, occupying the
eart (*h*), and sending their moisture to the
rough which they come in contact with
he air.

ıtline of the Animal Kingdom," Professor
most happily describes all these peculiari-
lerful indeed is the elaborate mechanism,"
, "employed to effect the double purpose
he respired fluid and feeding the helpless
these shells! Every filament of the bran-
ːxamined under a powerful microscope, is
ːovered with countless cilia in constant
sing, by their united efforts, powerful and
, which, sweeping over the surface of the
ːvards the mouth whatever floating animal-
tious particles, may be brought within the
ıction, and thus bring streams of nutritive
he very aperture through which they are
ıe stomach, the lips and labial fringes act-
ːs to admit or refuse entrance, as the matter
holesome or pernicious character."

has given the oyster a sensitive percep-
anges of light as the means of its protec-
many enemies it has to contend with; for
of an approaching boat is thrown forward
it, it closes the valves of its shell before
ı of the water can have reached it. This
ɪs easily studied in the marine vivary,
ter, with its beautiful cilia, more beautiful
e richest lace of a bride's wedding dress,
bject of great interest.

The oyster is an hermaphrodite animal, and hence its propagation is effected by self-produced eggs, which it bears within in the form of a greenish milky juice which it casts as spat in May, and which, as has already been stated, in this country is protected by wise and prudent acts of the Legislature. "The liquor in the lower shell of the oyster," says a writer in No. 587 of the "Family Herald," "if viewed through a microscope, will be found to contain multitudes of small oysters, covered with shells and swimming nimbly about—120 of which extend about an inch! Besides these young oysters, the liquor contains a variety of animalcules." Indeed, with the aid of a microscope one million of young have been discovered in a single oyster. Guarded by their two tender shells, these swim freely in the sea when ejected by the parent oyster, until, by means of a glutinous substance, they fix themselves so fast to some object that they can be separated only by force. These young are very soon able to produce others, many say at four months after their birth. When the oyster attains the size of a crown the shell is still very tender and thin; it is only after the second, third, or fourth year that it becomes fit for human food.

If we cannot answer the Fool's question in Lear, and "tell how an oyster makes his shell," we can, nevertheless, tell by his shell what is his age.

"A London oysterman," says a correspondent of No. 623 of the "Family Herald," "can tell the ages of his flock to a nicety. The age of an oyster is not to be found out by looking into its mouth. It bears its years upon its back. Everybody who has handled an oyster-shell must have observed that it seemed as if composed of successive layers or plates overlapping each other. These are technically termed ' shoots,' and each of them marks a year's growth; so that, by counting them, we can determine at a glance the year when the creature came into the world. Up to the time of its maturity, the shoots are regular and successive; but after that time they become irregular, and are piled one over the other, so that the shell becomes more and more thickened and bulky. Judging from the great thickness to which some oyster-shells have attained, this mollusk is capable, if left to its natural changes unmolested, of attaining a great age." Indeed, fossil oysters have been seen, of which each shell was nine inches thick, whence they may be concluded to have been more than 100 years old.

For the most part the offspring remains near the mother, which accounts for the large oyster banks or beds which are found in almost all the seas of the temperate and torrid zones, and which in some places have been known to attain such magnitude as to cause ships to be wrecked upon them. The lower stratum is necessarily lifeless, being pressed upon by the upper one, so that the oysters beneath are unable to open themselves, and are consequently deprived of food.

The immense propagation of the oyster may be understood from the fossil oyster bed near Reading, in Berkshire. These fossils have the entire shape, figure, and are of the same substance as our recent oyster-shells, and yet must have lain there from time immemorial. This bed occupies about six acres, forming

a stratum of about two feet in thickness. But the
largest fossil oyster banks are those raised by earth-
quakes along the western shores of South America,
which measure from sixty to eighty feet in depth, are
often forty miles in length, and in many places stretch
above two miles into the interior.

The Abbé Dicquemare, fond of trying experiments in
the spread of gastronomy, even to the stewing a mess of
Gemmaceæ, the *Gems* of our water-vivaries, till they had
something of the flavour of oysters, asserts that, when
in a state of liberty, oysters can move from one place
to another by suddenly admitting sea water into the
shell, which they are able to open and shut with extraordinary power and rapidity, whereby they produce a
strange sound; and this observation has been confirmed
by other naturalists, and is recorded as an ascertained
fact in several books of natural science. In like manner
they defend themselves against smaller animals, especially
against the spider crab, which constantly tries to pene-
trate into their half open shells. Much natural instinct
or foresight is also attributed to the oyster; in proof of
which I may name that, when in a position which is
exposed to the variations of the tide, oysters seem to be
aware that they remain for some hours without water,
and consequently provide it within their shells.

This makes such oysters far more fit to be conveyed
to a distance, than those taken nearer to the shore, which
evacuate the water, thus exposing themselves to the heat
of the sun, the cold, or an attack from their enemies;
and this, too, is the reason why Colchester or Pyfleet
oysters, packed at the beds, are in such request.

CHAPTER V.

THE OYSTER IN ITS NEW SETTLEMENT.

Dredging for Oysters; Oyster-beds and their formation; Sergius
Orata; Pliny the Elder; Baia and the Lucrine Sea; Roman
Epicurism and Gluttony; Martial and Horace, Cicero and
Seneca; Masticate Oysters, and do not bolt them whole;
Mediterranean and Atlantic Oysters; Agricola and the
Rutupians; Apicius Cœlius, Trajan, Pliny, and the Viva-
rium.

THE Oyster does not leave his home like the duckling,
upon the call of "come here and be killed." If he
is wanted, like Mrs. Glasse's hare, we must "first catch·
him." This is done by dredging, and this dredging for
oysters is performed by means of rakes and scrapers, on
which is fastened a bag of sail-cloth, leather, or net-work.
These are lowered into the sea by means of ropes and
chains, and are dragged along its bottom by boats in full
sail, or by rowing-boats. When the net or scraper is
drawn to the surface, the oysters are immediately
separated from all else which may be swept up. These
oysters are then stowed away and sent up to market in
due course. But it is not of these that are formed the
new settlements or oyster-beds, which I am about to
describe.

These oyster-beds are cavities or reservoirs which com-
municate with the sea by means of canals, and are placed
in such manner that the level beds remain dry when

the tide is high.   These beds are made with sand-stones
or other hewn stones; and the water is kept in or let
out at low tide by means of locks, or traps, as may be
most readily effected.

At some periods, however, the water is kept in for
many days, or even weeks together.   In the latter case
the oyster becomes, for the most part, very tender, and
green and fat, because the stagnant water promotes the
germination of those microscopical spores of marine
plants, which always abound in natural sea-water, and
upon which it delights to feed.   These reservoirs, therefore, are not only the means of preserving them for sale
but of purifying them from the muddy odour which they
have imbibed at sea, and which indicates them to be hard
and devoid of that luscious and somewhat gastronomic
quality so much prized by the world at large.

The bottom and sides of these caves or reservoirs are
paved with stones and thick layers of sand, to keep them
free from all mud, which is not only very injurious to
the animal, but sure to harbour its enemies; and great
care is also observed not to admit too great a flow o
water at one time, as that might drive particles of sand
into the shells.   When the reservoir is properly prepared
the oysters are placed in their natural position—the fla
side being upwards, in a sloping or horizontal direction
The more care that is taken in keeping their beds clear
and free from mud, by washing the sides of the reservoirs, pouring water over the oysters, especially those
which are dry, and removing the dead ones, which can
be recognised by their shells being open, the better; for
the more valuable will they be as human food, both as

to profit and condition, and the more appreciated by the gastronomic million, who hail the oyster season as does a sportsman the advent of grouse and partridges, hares and pheasants.

The oysters, which are thus preserved, cleaned, nursed, and fattened are taken from their beds at the low tide when the water is out.

There are doubts, various and conflicting, as to whether oysters contained in reservoirs, where the water is changed each successive tide, are not on that account preferable to those which exist in the same water for two weeks at a time. I give a decided prefer- ence to the latter, though the water must be kept very clean by constant care and attention to the removal of the dead, the decomposition of which would otherwise, out for the frequent change of water, seriously affect the health of the whole settlement, by an accumulation of sulphuretted hydrogen, with a smell like that emitted by the Thames and other drainage rivers in the dog- days. These oysters slip down the human throat divine with a tenderness and sublime relish which no words can describe.

Let me pass over, for the nonce, the mode of packing and sending them to the interior. Thanks to the rail- ways, the gastronomical delight of oyster eating is now secured to many who for years scarcely knew what an oyster meant in its entire freshness and best qualities.

Sergius Orata, as Pliny the Elder tells us in the eighty-ninth book of his invaluable Natural History, and, as we have already stated, first conceived the idea of planting oysters in beds. This epicure had large reservoirs made at Baia, where he gathered thousands of these mollusks. Not far from these oyster-beds rose a palace in which the wealthy Roman used to assemble his choicest friends and feast with them the whole day and night. Oysters occupied the place of honour on the table of Sergius Orata; at every feast thousands of them were consumed. Satiated, but not yet satisfied, these gourmets were in the habit of adjourning into an adjoining room, where they relieved the stomach of its load by artificial means, and then returned to indulge again their appetite with a fresh supply of oysters.

Strange as it may appear to us in the nineteenth century, this custom was universal amongst the wealthy of Imperial Rome, Cæsar himself often indulging in it when the repast was to his taste; and ladies, the cream of the cream of that luxurious period, carried about with them peacocks' feathers and other dainty throat ticklers for the purpose, when they anticipated a more luxurious feed than usual.

Who amongst us cares to eat white-bait in the crowded city? When the mood seizes us, do not we take boat and proceed up or down the river, as the whim dictates? The old Roman had no white-bait and the oyster to him was therefore doubly welcome. To him the journey to his marine villa, by water or land, as with us, added but a zest to the anticipated treat. In the Bay of Naples is a smaller bay close to its most north-western point, bounded on the west by the pretty town of Baia and its hot wells, and on the north-east by the no less charming town of Pozzuoli. These little bays on the Italian coasts are dignified by the name of seas by the writers of classical antiquity, and round the headland of Baia, to the north, in the open Mediterranean—the Tyrrhenian Sea—just such another bay, the present Lago di Fusaro, was called the Lucrine Sea, with its far-famed oyster-beds, easy of access from Baia and Pozzuoli, both situated in a charming country. Here, close to the Lucrine, under a clear sky, surrounded by a delightful atmosphere, were situated the country houses of the more wealthy Romans, where, far away from business and the noise and turmoil of the forum, these accomplished disciples of Epicurus, without fear or care, used to give themselves up to the delights of the table. Here they tasted the little-shelled oysters which Martial liked so much, and which, but a few hours previously to being served up, had been gathered on the sea-shore.

Gastronomic annals mention the names of some of these dainty persons who daily swallowed several hundreds of oysters; but Vitellius in this respect beat them all. That emperor, it is said, ate oysters four times a day, and at each meal swallowed neither more nor less than 1200 of them. Seneca himself, who so admirably praises the charms of poverty, yet left prodigious wealth behind him; Seneca the wise and moderate, ate several hundreds of them every week.

"Oyster, so dear to people of taste!" he exclaims; "thou dost but excite instead of satisfying the appetite, never causing indisposition, not even when eaten to excess; for thou art easy of digestion, and the stomach yields thee back with facility." Cicero did not hesitate to confess that he had a special predilection for oysters;

but he adds, that he could renounce them without any difficulty; which, by the way, he might as well have told to the Marines, if they were in existence in his day, for all the credence this remark of his has gained from posterity.

We prefer Horace, who in every passage honestly makes known his love for oysters, and eats them himself with as much gusto as he extols them to others. Carefully, too, does he note down from whom he procured them, and the name of the famous gourmet who at the first bite was able to tell whether an oyster came from Circe or the Lucrine Sea, or from any part of Natolia. The ancients, our teachers in all arts, but especially in æsthetics, did not bolt the oyster, but masticated it. With true Epicurean tact, they always extracted the full enjoyment out of the good things set before them. Not so we; most of us now bolt them; but this is a mistake, for the oyster has a much finer flavour, and is far more nourishing, when well masticated.

"Those who wish to enjoy this delicious restorative in its utmost perfection," says Dr. Kitchener, "must *eat* it the moment it is opened, with its own gravy in the under shell; if not *eaten* absolutely alive, its flavour and spirit are lost. The true lover of an oyster will have some regard for the feelings of his little favourite, and contrive to detach the fish from the shell so dexterously that the oyster is hardly conscious he has been ejected from his lodging till he *feels the teeth* of the piscivorous gourmet tickling him to death."

The Romans needed not even the use of their teeth to tell from whence the oyster came; a mere look sufficed to distinguish it, as may be seen in the following lines ascribed to Lucilius.

> "When I but see the oyster's shell,
> I look and recognize the river, marsh or mud,
> Where it was raised."

Nor was this so very difficult a matter, for the shell, no less than the animal itself, as has already been shown, exhibits the nature of the food upon which the oyster has fed.

In Italy and Gaul it was for a long time a matter of dispute, which country produced the best oysters. At that time the Lucrine Sea maintained the superiority; but Pliny preferred those from Circe. "According to my opinion," he says, "the most delicious and most tender oysters are those from Circe."

At last, however, the preference was given to those of Britain, which under the wise administration of Julius Agricola had conformed to the manners and customs of her conquerors, and there no longer was need of dispute as to whether the Mediterranean oysters of Italy or Gaul should have the precedence. The little watery pulpy dabs, which had hitherto delighted the conquerors of the world, were cast aside in disgust. They had found a real oyster at last, and the insignificant and flavourless bivalves of the coasts of Italy ceased to be in demand. From that time, on the shores of the Atlantic, thousands of slaves were employed in procuring the oysters, which in Rome were paid for by their weight in gold. The expenses were so great that the censors felt themselves obliged to interfere. Not content with getting their oysters from distant shores, they had means

by which to preserve them for some time in hot weather;
for which purpose, as we see in the Pompeian model-
house at the Crystal Palace, their domiciles were
furnished with a receptacle for water; for with those
famous epicures the water-vivary was an essential
necessary for the preservation of living fish, and all that
was necessary was to substitute sea-water for fresh.
Probably by some such means, Apicius Cœlius, who
must not be confounded with the writer of a book of
cookery which bears his name, sent Trajan, when that
emperor was in the country of the Parthians, oysters,
which when received were as fresh as they ever could
be eaten when just taken from their beds; and Pliny
even believed that the journey had proved beneficial to
their flavour.

CHAPTER VI.

THE OYSTER ON ITS TRAVELS.

The Isle of Sheppey, the Medway, and Whitstable; Milton, Queenborough, Rochester, and Faversham Oysters; Colchester and Essex Beds; Edinburgh Pandores and Aberdours; Dublin Carlingfords and Powldoodies; Poole and its Oyster-bank; Cornish Oysters and the Helford Beds; Poor Tyacke, and How he was Done; Dredgers and their Boats; Auld Reekie's Civic Ceremonials; Song of the Oyster; its Voyage to Market, and Journey by Coach and Rail.

WHO that has travelled by water from London Bridge to Herne Bay—and who among us who live within the sound of Bow bells has not?—should the trip have been made in the beginning of August, but must have noticed, after having passed the Isle of Sheppey, a little fishing-town to his right, in East Swale Bay, raising its head out of the river like a joyous child dressed in its gayest attire, anticipating a long-looked-for holiday? It is the 4th of August, and its holiday is at hand, for to-morrow the oyster season begins; and the town is Whitstable, in Kent, standing out gaily with its bright flags and pennons in beautiful relief from the low marshy soil by which it is surrounded. Then, too, the dredgers, in their picturesque costume, add greatly to the gay appearance of the place, whilst some seventy or eighty vessels lying in the offing bespeak the importance of the oyster traffic between it and the Great Metropolis. What the Lucrine was to the citizen of Rome is the estuary of the Medway with the Swale to the citizen of London. The "Natives" obtained at Milton are in the highest repute, and consumed in every part of England; nor are the Faversham, Queenborough, and Rochester denizens less so; nor, indeed, any of the "breedy creatures" which are raised in the other beds of the Swale or the Medway.

The trade in oysters, as we have seen, has been an object of consideration in England for many ages, and now ranks in importance with the herring, pilchard, and other fisheries. The excellence of our oysters made the formation of artificial beds an object of attention soon after the Roman conquest; and the Kentish and Essex beds show a pedigree in consequence much older than that of the noble descendant of any Norman adventurer who came over with the Conqueror, claiming, on this head alone, precedence for our "Natives" amongst all the oysters of the known world. But Britain is the boasted land of liberty, and the "Natives" of one part of her coast boldly assert their equality with the "Natives" of any other. If London delights in Milton and Colchester oysters, Edinburgh has her "whispered Pandores" and Aberdours, and Dublin her Carlingfords* and "Powldoodies of Burran;" whilst all

* The Carlingford oyster is the best in Ireland; a black-bearded fellow, delicate and of fine flavour, to be eaten in Dublin alternately with the Redbank oyster, at a magnificent establishment in Sackville Street, and to be washed down with

round our shores each locality boasts of its own "Natives" as the best oysters in the land. Poole points proudly to her oyster-bank, and tells miraculous tales of her fishery, and of the number of oysters she sends to the London market, besides those which are pickled at sea for the export trade to lands where a fresh oyster is still a luxury unknown. The Poole fishermen who open oysters in their boats for pickling are compelled, by an Act of the Legislature, to throw the shells on the strand, and these, in the course of time, have formed a strong barrier against the waves of the sea at the flow of the tide, having the appearance of an island at high-water; and, simple as it is, such is the sole construction of this celebrated breakwater.

I cannot be expected to take the reader on a voyage of discovery all round the coast, nor to the Channel Islands, to taste the oysters which Providence has spread out for our enjoyment with such a lavish hand. But there is one little spot on the shores of Cornwall which I cannot pass over, because from it came one of the colonies on the banks of the Thames, from which the Whitstable boats still draw their annual supply. Into Mount's Bay the Helford River, upon which stands the little town of Helstone, empties itself, opposite Mount St. Michael's, into the sea, and in the estuary of that little river, a person of the name of Tyacke, within the memory of the " oldest

alternate draughts of brown stout. The Hibernian will tell you that even our Natives are inferior to these. He is right in his patriotism, but wrong in his assertion. How often do our prejudices trip up our judgment!

inhabitant," rented certain oyster-beds, famous amongst
Cornish gourmets for a breed of oysters, which, it is
said, the Phœnicians, "a long time ago," had discovered
to be infinitely preferable to the watery things they got
at home. These Helford oysters are regularly brought
to London; but when Tyacke rented the beds they were
unknown to the good citizens who frequented the oyster taverns, of which the Cock in Fleet Street is but a
last lingering type. Determined to make his venture,
Tyacke loaded a fishing smack with the best produce of
his beds, and coasted along the southern shores, till
passing round the Isle of Thanet he found himself in the
Mouth of the Thames. Little did the elated oyster
dredger think that that Mouth would swallow up the
whole of his cargo; but so it came to pass. It had long
been evident to those on board that oysters that travel,
no less than men, must have rations allowed on the
voyage, if they are to do credit to the land of their birth.
Now the voyage had been long and tedious, and the
oysters had not been fed, so Tyacke got into his boat,
and obtained an interview with the owner of the spot at
which it touched land. He asked permission to lay
down his oysters, and feed them. This was granted, and
after a few days the spores of *ulva latissima* and *entero-
morpha*, and of the host of delicate fibrous plants which
there abound, and all of which are the oyster's great
delight, made the whole green and fat, and in the finest
condition for reshipment. Four days, it is said, will
suffice to make a lean oyster, on such a diet, both green
and plump; and Tyacke, joyful at the improvement
which he daily witnessed, let his stock feed on for a

week. It was towards evening that he bethought himself, as the tide was out, that if he meant to reach Billingsgate by the next morning, it would be wise to reship his oysters before turning in for the night. The boat was lowered; but, as he attempted to land, he was warned off by the owner of the soil, who stood there with several fierce looking fellows, armed with cutlasses and fowling-pieces, evidently anticipating the Cornishman's intention, and determined to frustrate it at all hazards.

" What do you want here ?" he asked of Tyacke.

" The oysters I put down to feed," was the reply. " They were placed there by your permission, and now I am anxious to reship them, to be in time for to-morrow's market."

" True," replied the Kentishman, " I gave you leave to lay down the oysters and feed them, but not a word was said about reshipping them. Where they are, there they stay; and if you persist in trespassing, I shall know what to do."

Poor Tyacke found himself much in the predicament of many a flat who has been picked up by a sharp. A century ago law was not justice, nor justice law. Perhaps it may not even be so now; and the story of the lawyer who ate the oyster in dispute, and gave each of the disputants a shell, may hold as good in our day as it did in that when the author of the "Beggar's Opera" put it into verse.

The demand for oysters, wherever it exists along our coasts, creates a profitable source of employment to a class of men who necessarily become experienced seamen; and dredging for oysters is carried on in fleets, as the beds mostly lie within a comparatively small space. The boats, which are about fifteen feet long, usually carry a man and a boy, or two men. The dredge is about eighteen pounds weight, and is required to be heavier on a hard than on a soft bottom, and each boat is usually provided with two dredges.

In former days the commencement of the dredging season was held sufficiently important to entitle it to a civic ceremonial, at least such was the wont of the municipal authorities of " Auld Reekie," who also paid a particular regard both as to the supply and the price of the '" breedy creatures" furnished to the good citizens of Edinburgh. The "Feast of Shells" was ushered in by the municipality of the ancient city making, for provosts and bailiffs, a somewhat perilous voyage to the oyster-beds in the Frith of Forth; and though the solemnity of wedding the Frith formed no part of the chief magistrate's office, as wedding the Adriatic with a gold ring did that of the Doge of Venice, the welkin was made to ring, as three cheers from all present uprose and announced the lifting of the first dredge upon the deck of the civic barge.

There is something poetical and pretty in the idea, which once prevailed, that the oyster was a lover of music, and as the fishermen trolled their dredging nets they sang,

"To charm the spirits of the deep."

The old ballad in use is still found in the mouth of

many a hardy seaman as he pursues his toil to the
melodious words—

> " The herring loves the merry moonlight,
> The mackerel loves the wind,
> But the oyster loves the dredger's song,
> For he comes of a gentle kind."

Raised out of his native waters, the oyster makes the
voyage to the first station in his destined travels in the
company of those to whom long and kindred ties have
bound him, on board the smack upon the deck of which
they were jointly landed from the deep; and during
the whole voyage, if it prove a long one, he is atten-
tively supplied with refreshing water, so that when the
smack lays alongside the wharf at which he is to part
company with his captors, he is still as lively as when
they first took him as a passenger on board.

Arrived in port, the oyster first truly becomes sensible
of the miseries of slavery. Shovelled into sacks, or cast
anyhow into carts and handbarrows, he may consider
himself fortunate if a kindly hand but extends to him, in
his great necessity, a drink of water impregnated with
salt, instead of his own delicious beverage from the sea.
Yet this is a cruelty which should be avoided wherever
sea-water can be obtained, because it is neither the salt
nor the water which sustains the oyster's life, but the
spores of vegetation which abound in the sea, and by
mixing salt with fresh water we destroy even the life of
the incipient fresh-water plants which the latter contains. It is as great a mockery as when Grumio pro-
poses to give the famished Katherine the mustard
without the brawn, and need no longer exist if oyster

dealers, who cannot obtain sea-water, w
themselves with the prepared salts for the
production of artificial sea-water, the r
preparation of which is thus given in N
" Family Herald :"—

" For ten gallons it requires, sulphate of magn
sulphate of lime, 2¾ ounces ; chloride of sodiu
chloride of magnesia, 6 ounces ; chloride of
ounce ; bromide of magnesium, 21 grains ; ca
21 grains."

This should be allowed to stand expose
a strong sunlight for a fortnight before it i:
which time a few growing plants of *enterom*
should be introduced to throw off spores.
cost about one shilling each in London
then, when under the microscope, will be
tain a confervoid vegetable growth, which
ishing a food for the oyster as the spores
its ocean bed.   Oysters laid down in a lar
covered with this water will continue to 1
for months ; and it was to some such meth
the Romans were indebted for the preser
oysters in inland stews.   On no account sl
flour, or any such *dead* stuff, be added
serves to make the water foul and the oys
When oysters are to travel by coach o1
usually dispatched in barrels.   Where tl
packed at the beds, as the Colchester
barrelled oysters" are, they should not be
wanted for the table, as they will keep go
for a week or ten days ; for being carefull

ıot to spill the water each carries in a reservoir of
Nature's providing, they need no other viaticum for the
ourney.

The moment an oyster in the barrel opens its mouth
t dies, because there is nothing in the barrel to sustain
ts life. It is therefore as well, on the receipt of the
ittle cask, to open it at once by removing the top and
;he first hoop, and then to place the top on the upper-
nost layer of oysters, keeping it in position by the
iddition of some heavy weight, which causes the staves
o spread and stand erect; and as the layers of oysters
ire required for the table, it is only necessary each time
o replace the top and the weight to a similar position
o keep the remainder fresh for a few days. But the
rue lover of an oyster will have some regard for his
ittle favourite. Sea-water may be had in London and
ither large towns for sixpence per gallon, and when
hat cannot be procured the pound packet of salts,
iccording to the recipé we have given, will not cost
nore than eighteen-pence at any chemist's, and that
[uantity will produce three gallons of artificial sea-
vater. Thus provided, unpack the barrel, and spread
iut the oysters in a large flat earthenware dish, just
:overing them with water, and you may keep them for
nany weeks as fresh as when they first left their beds.

CHAPTER VII.

THE OYSTER AT ITS JOURNEY'S END.

Oyster Stalls; How to Open the Oyster; an Oyster Supper;
Beer, Wines, and Spirits; Roasted, Fried, Stewed, and Scol-
loped Oysters; Oyster Soup, and Oyster Sauce; Broiled
Oysters; Oyster Pie; Oyster Toast; Oyster Patties; Oyster
Powder; Pickled Oysters; Oyster Loaves; Oyster Omelet;
Cabbage, Larks, and Oysters; and Frogs and Oysters.

> "If where Fleet Ditch with muddy current flows
> You chance to roam, where oyster-tubs in rows
> Are ranged beside the posts, there stay thy haste,
> And with the savoury fish indulge thy taste."—GAY.

I AM writing for the Million, and the least the Million
can do in return is every one to buy a copy of my book,
and bid everybody to recommend everybody to do the
same. The Fleet Ditch, which was once in the centre
of the old Fleet Market, has disappeared since Gay wrote
the lines I have just quoted, and now forms the great
sewer of Farringdon Street; but with the Ditch have
not disappeared the oyster-stalls; they have only
changed their locality, and, like the Wandering Jew,
have turned up in the most out-of-the-way places,
where nobody would expect to find them. I know
what stall-oysters are; for when I was a school-boy
many and oft is the time I spent my pennies, on the sly,
at a stall behind the old cathedral that just abutted the
ancient Market Cross. The maiden that opened them

had clean white hands—for, boy as I was, I could not have endured a baronet's hand to open oysters for me; for—

"The damsel's knife the gaping shell commands,
While the salt liquor streams between her hands."

Never have I eaten finer oysters than those, fresh almost within a few hours from the placid Solent, upon which now the palace of Osborne looks down, and calls forth the heartfelt prayer of "God bless the Queen," as we pass beneath the grass-covered slopes, reminding every Wykehamist of the founder's motto, "Manners maketh Men;" for Her Majesty is the tenant of Wykeham's College, and his arms and motto are carved upon the gates of the Queen's royal residence of Osborne.

Yes, "Manners maketh Men" no less than *Honores nutant Mores*, as the punster told the great Sir Thomas More, when he stood so high in favour with Henry VIII., and was just appointed Treasurer of the Exchequer. It is not riches that make man, any more than they need change him; and if there is any good gift of Providence more than another which teaches equality, it will not be far from the mark to say it is the Oyster. You cannot eat the oyster in greater perfection than at a street-stall, because, as the capital of the owner is small, so, too, is the stock; and, to be sure of a rapid sale, it must also be well and carefully selected, and therefore does not need the announcement we read in many a by-way one passes along, where "the tale of a tub" would seem to contradict it: "Oysters fresh every

day." The poor man has no need to bid his cook,
like his wealthy neighbour, buy real sea-water, or
salts for the preparation of artificial sea-water, for the
preservation of his oysters. There are thousands of
hands outstretched to receive his nimble penny, and to
give him in return oysters as fine as any which can
grace the table of the wealthiest in the land. To me it
is a treat to stand by and see how rapidly oyster after
oyster disappears down the capacious throat of some
stalwart son of toil, and to think that my favourite
health-giving mollusk, in every one that is swallowed,
is adding strength and muscle to those upon whom we
so greatly depend for the nation's wealth and prosperity.

People generally, however, are somewhat indifferent
about the manner of opening oysters, and the time of
eating them after they are opened; yet nothing deserves
more consideration at the hands of your true oyster-eater.
The oyster should be eaten the moment it is opened, if
eaten raw, with its own liquor in the under shell, as we
have already stated on the very highest of all gastronomical authorities. It is well worth a little practice to
learn to open the oyster oneself, for a bungling opera-
tor injures our little favourite, and baulks the expectant
appetite by his unsightly incisions. I learnt the art
years ago in one of the Midland counties, where Christmas-eve would scarce be Christmas-eve, without an
oyster supper. Let me sketch the scene. In the centre
of the table, covered with a clean white cloth up to the
top hoop, stands the barrel of oysters, a kindly remem-
brance from a friend, and the more kind because oysters
are not found in fresh-water streams. Each gentleman at

table finds an oyster-knife and a clean coarse towel by the side of his plate, and he is expected to open oysters for himself and the lady seated by his side, unless she is wise enough to open them for herself. By the side of every plate is the *panis ostrearius*, the oyster-loaf made and baked purposely for the occasion, and all down the centre of the table, interspersed with vases of bright holly and evergreens, are plates filled with pats of butter, or lemons cut in half, and as many vinegar and pepper castors as the establishment can furnish. As the attendance of servants at such gatherings is usually dispensed with, bottled Bass or Guinness, or any equally unsophisticated pale ale or porter, is liberally provided; and where the means allow, light continental wines, such as Chablis, Sauterne, Mousseux, Marsault or Medoc, still Champagne, Moselle, or any light Rhenish wine, and failing any of these, Madeira or Sherry, are placed upon the table. In this list is contained the names of such wines only as are best suited to enhance the taste of the oyster, and to assist digestion. Of spirits, only good English gin, genuine Schiedam, or Irish or Scotch whisky, are admissible, as rum and brandy, taken upon oysters, will almost always be sure to make them indigestible; and liqueurs are quite out of place.

At some of these oyster suppers, oysters roasted in the shell are brought in "hot and hot," and dishes of fried, stewed, and scolloped oysters follow each other in quick succession, and even oyster patties are sometimes introduced; but I hold up both hands against an American innovation which is creeping in, and introducing crabs

E

and lobsters, and mixed pickles, and other fo
the *carte* on such an occasion.

The mention of these various dishes of dre
reminds me of my promise at starting, to g
rections as to the proper mode of cooking tl
begin : —

1. *The Fried Oyster.*—It is the most common or
in its own shell ; but as it frequently takes the
when just fried, it is better to make use of anot
porcelain one.   The beard is taken off, the oy
from its shell, and with the liquor it still conta
the vessel prepared for it, with some good butter
san cheese, and pepper, and thus it is put into tl
the gridiron, and when it has turned a little brow
juice is poured on it, after which it may be serve
no Parmesan, good dry Cheshire, or even brea
desirable.   The largest and finest oysters should
this purpose ; and many persons fry oysters by si
them to simmer in their own shells for a coup
when they take them out and lay them on a c
beard them, and then flour them, put them into l
fry them to a delicate brown.

2. *The Oyster roasted in its own shell.*—Open t
fully, so as not to lose any of its own liquor, add
and pepper, according to taste, place it up(
over a fierce clear fire, and serve up " hot and l
succession.   Bachelors may manage to dress o
way by placing them betwen the bars of the grate
adding the butter and pepper as they eat them.

3. *Stewed Oysters.*—Open the oysters, and put
a stew-pan with a little beaten mace ; thicken
and butter ; boil it three or four minutes ; put
of cream ; put in the oysters, and shake them
pan, but do not let them boil.   Serve them in a sr
or if for one person only in a soup-plate.

4. *Scolloped Oysters.*—Open the oysters, put them in a basin, with their own liquor ; put them into a small deep dish, or some of them, if preferred, into scollop shells ; strew over them a few crumbs of bread, and lay a slice of butter on them ; then more oysters, bread crumbs, and a slice of butter on the top ; put them into a Dutch-oven to brown, and serve them up.

5. *Oyster Soups.*—(Each of the following is calculated for one person).

(*a*). *The English Soup.*—Take one pound of good lean beef, half a pound of raw lean ham, much parsley, and carrot roots, and a few onions ; cut all in very small pieces, and burnish it into a dark-brownish colour with spices, bay-leaves, whole pepper and butter : after having boiled this with water for five hours, pour it through a hair sieve, and then put to it a little brown flour, and two ounces of Sherry or Madeira, and after having boiled again for an hour, take all the fat clean off, and put into it the oysters with their beards and liquor, and with cayenne pepper; all this is to be boiled up again, and then served. This soup is to be recommended, especially in winter when it is very cold. For invalids, the wine, spices, and pepper are omitted. This soup is valuable for convalescents, being very strengthening and nourishing.

(*b*). *The American Soup.*—Take half a pint of good fresh milk, or cream if possible ; three ounces of good butter; boil this together, beat it up with the yolks of three eggs, and put into it six or twelve oysters with their beards and liquor ; boil this up again, and in serving it up put into it a little cayenne pepper and a few drops of lemon juice. This soup is delicate ; but no prejudice ! Everybody must try it first. For invalids, butter, eggs, and pepper are omitted.

(*c*). *The Holstein Soup.*—Take good beef-stock, one-eighth of a pound of Sherry or Madeira, burnt flour, and proceed as with (*a*) ; and then beat it up with the yolks of two or three eggs. The beard and the liquor must always be made use of, as they impart the strongest flavour of the oyster.)

6. *Oyster Sauce.*—I cannot do better than copy Dr. Kitchener's

valuable recipe for making oyster sauce, which was one c
the great luxuries at the table of that celebrated gastronome :—
"Choose plump and juicy natives for this purpose ; do not tak
them out of their shells till you put them into the stew-par
To make good oyster sauce for half a dozen hearty fish-eater:
you cannot have less than three or four dozen oysters ; sav
their liquor, strain it, and put it and them into a stew-pan
as soon as they boil, and the fish plump, take them off the fir
and pour the contents of the stew-pan into a sieve over a clea
basin ; wash the stew-pan out with hot water, and put into it tl
strained liquor, with about an equal quantity of milk, and abo1
two and a half ounces of butter, with which you have well rubbe
a large table-spoonful of tlour; give it a boil up, and pour it throug
a sieve into a basin, that the sauce may be quite smooth, a1
then back again into the saucepan ; now shave the oysters, a1
(if you have the honour of making sauce for "a Committee
Taste," take away the gristly part also) put in only the soft pe
of the oysters ; if they are very large, cut them in half, and s
them by the fire to keep hot ; 'if they boil after, they will t
come hard.' If you have not liquor enough, add a little melt
butter, or cream, or milk beat up with the yolk of an egg (tl
must not be put in till the sauce is done). Some barbarc
cooks add pepper, or mace, the juice or peel of a lemon, hor
radish essence of anchovy, cayenne, etc. ; plain sauces are o1
to taste of the ingredients from which they derive their nan
It will very much heighten the flavour of this sauce to pound t
soft part of half a dozen unboiled oysters ; rub it througl
hair sieve, and then stir it into the sauce. This essence of oyst
and for some palates a few grains of cayenne, is the only addit:
we recommend."

Notwithstanding Dr. Kitchener's objection to t
introduction of extraneous substances by "*barbar(*
cooks," because *de Gustibus*, as the adage of "t
apple and the onion" has already reminded me,
always a matter not to be disputed, I shall add Ale:

Soyer's "barbarous" method of preparing oyster sauce, which was introduced by him at the Reform Club in 1852 :—

"Mix three ounces of butter in a stewpan with two ounces of flour, then blanch and beard three dozen oysters, put the oysters into another stewpan, add beards and liquor to the flour and butter, with a pint and a half of milk, a teaspoonful of salt, half a salt-spoonful of cayenne, two cloves, half a blade of mace, and six peppercorns ; place it over the fire, keep stirring, and boil it ten minutes, then add a tablespoonful of essence of anchovies, and one of Harvey sauce ; pass it through a hair-sieve over the oysters ; make the whole very hot without boiling, and serve. A less quantity may be made, using less proportions."

He also gives the following :—

"Put a pint of white sauce into a stew-pan, with the liquor and beards of three dozen oysters (as above), six peppercorns, two cloves, and half a blade of mace ; boil it ten minutes, then add a spoonful of essence of anchovies, a little cayenne and salt if required ; pass it through a tammy, or hair-sieve, over the oysters, as in the last."

This is somewhat similar to that given in that most useful pennyworth "The Family Herald Economical Cookery," which is also preferred by many, and is as follows :—

"Simmer the oysters in their own liquor till they are plump : strain off the liquor through a sieve, wash the oysters clean, and beard them; put them into a saucepan, and pour the liquor over them, taking care you do not pour in any of the sediment ; add a blade of mace, a quarter of a lemon, a spoonful of anchovy liquor, and a bit of horseradish ; boil it up gently, then take out the horseradish, the mace, and the lemon, the juice of which must be squeezed into the sauce. Now add some thick melted butter, toss it together, and boil it up."

I am bound to admit that my own opinion coincides with that of Dr. Kitchener, and would only add that no trouble is too great to render the sauce perfectly smooth, and that no niggard hand should have the supplying it for the table.

6. *Large Oysters Broiled.*—Take the largest and finest oysters you can get, such as you find in the West of England and in America; clean the gridiron as if a fairy had done the work for Cinderella in her sleep; rub the bars with *fresh* butter, and set it over a clear fire, quite free from smoke; then place the oysters upon it, being careful not to let them burn, and when done on one side, turn them quickly on the other with a fork. Put some fresh butter in the bottom of a hot dish, and lay the oysters upon it, sprinkling them slightly with pepper. They must be served quite hot with fried parsley.

7. *Oyster Pie.*—Having buttered the inside of a deep dish, spread a rich paste over the sides and round the edge, but not at the bottom. The oysters should be as large and fine as possible, and when opened drain off part of the liquor from them. Put them into a pan, and season them with pepper, salt, and spice, and stir them well with the seasoning. Pour the oysters with their liquor into the dish, and strew over them the yolks of eggs chopped fine and grated bread. Roll out the lid of the pie, and put it on, crimping the edges handsomely. Take a small sheet of paste, cut it into a square, and roll it up. Cut it with a sharp knife into the form of a double tulip. Make a slit in the centre of the upper crust, and stick the tulip in it. Cut out some large leaves of paste, and lay them on the lid, and bake the pie in a quick oven.

Another way of preparing this favourite French dish

is this, communicated to me by a lady of some experience in matters gastronomical :—

" Having buttered the inside of a deep dish, line it with puff-paste rolled out rather thick, and prepare another sheet of paste for the lid. Put a clean towel into the dish (folded so as to support the lid) and then put on the lid ; set it into the oven, and bake the paste well. When done, remove the lid, and take out the folded towel. While the paste is baking, prepare the oysters. Having picked off carefully any bits of shell that may be found about them, lay them in a sieve and drain off the liquor into a pan. Put the oysters into a skillet or stew-pan, with barely enough of the liquor to keep them from burning. Season them with whole pepper, blades of mace, some grated nutmeg, and some grated lemon-peel, (the yellow rind only,) and a little finely minced celery. Then add a large portion of fresh butter, divided into bits, and very slightly dredged with flour. Let the oysters simmer over the fire, but do not allow them to come to a boil, as that will shrivel them. Next beat the yolks only, of three, four, or five eggs, (in proportion to the size of the pie,) and stir the beaten egg into the stew a few minutes before you take it from the fire. Keep it warm till the paste is baked. Then carefully remove the lid of the pie ; and replace it, after you have filled the dish with the oysters and gravy.

" The lid of the pie may be ornamented with a wreath of leaves cut out of paste, and put on before baking. In the centre, place a paste-knot or flower.

" Oyster pies are generally eaten warm ; but they are very good cold."

8. *Oyster Toast.*—Cut four slices of bread, pare off the crusts, and toast them. Butter the toast on both sides. Then select a dozen of fine fat and plump oysters, and mince them ; place them thickly between the slices of toast, seasoning them with cayenne pepper. Beat the yolks of four eggs, and mix them with half-a-pint of cream, adding, if thought necessary, a few

blades of mace. Put the whole into a saucepan, and set it over the fire to simmer till thick ; but do not allow it to boil, and stir it well, lest it should curdle. When it is *near* boiling heat, take it off and pour it over the toast.

9. *Oyster Patties.*—" Roll out puff-paste a quarter of an inch thick," says Dr. Kitchener, " cut it into squares with a knife, sheet eight or ten patty pans, put upon each a bit of bread the size of half a walnut ; roll out another layer of paste of the same thickness, cut it as above, wet the edge of the bottom paste, and put on the top, pare them round to the pan, and notch them about a dozen times with the back of the knife, rub them lightly with yolk of egg, bake them in a hot oven about a quarter of an hour : when done, take a thin slice off the top, then, with a small knife or spoon, take out the bread and the inside paste, leaving the outside quite entire : then parboil two dozen of large oysters, strain them from their liquor, wash, beard, and cut them into four, put them into a stew-pan with an ounce of butter rolled in flour, half a gill of good cream, a little grated lemon-peel, the oyster liquor free from sediment, reduced by boiling to one half, some cayenne pepper, salt, and a tea-spoonful of lemon-juice ; stir it over a fire five minutes, and fill the patties."

10. *Oyster Powder.*—Open the oysters carefully, so as not to cut them, except in dividing the gristle which attaches the shells ; put them into a mortar, and when you have got as many as you can conveniently pound at once, add about two drachms of salt to a dozen oysters ; pound them and rub them through the back of a hair sieve, and put them into the mortar again, with as much flour (which has been previously thoroughly dried) as will make them into a paste ; roll the paste out several times, and lastly, flour it, and roll it out the thickness of a half-crown, and divide it into pieces about one inch square ; lay them in a Dutch oven, where they will dry so gently as not to get burned ; turn them every half hour, and when they begin to dry, crumble them. They will take about four hours to dry; then pound them fine, sift them, and put them into dry bottles

and seal them. Three dozens of natives require seven ounces and a half of flour to make them into a paste weighing eleven ounces, or when dried and powdered, six and a half ounces. To make half a pint of sauce, put one ounce of butter into a stew-pan with three drachms of oyster powder, and six table-spoonfuls of milk ; set it on a slow fire, stir it till it boils, and season it with salt. This makes an excellent sauce for fish, fowls, or rump steaks. Sprinkled on bread and butter, it makes a good sandwich. But only use plump juicy natives in the preparation.

11. *Pickled Oysters* are mostly used for salads when no fresh oysters can be got. Take good wine, or Tarragon vinegar, some onions cut in pieces, some slices of lemon, some spices, whole pepper, bay leaves, and salt. Boil this together, and whilst boiling put the oysters into it, and let the whole boil up once more. Put the result into bottles with a little good oil, and, tied over with bladder, it will keep for a long time.

However, pickled oysters also appear as a supper dish, when they are thus prepared :—

Take two dozen oysters ; strain the liquor ; add three blades of mace, six peppercorns, a little grated lemon peel, and one or two bay leaves ; boil the liquor, and, when boiling, add the oysters for two minutes. When cold, strain off the liquor; place the oysters in a small dish, and garnish with parsley. According to this rate of ingredients the dish may be made to suit the number of guests likely to partake of it.

12. *Oyster Loaves.*—Make an oval hole in the top of some rasped French rolls, and scrape out all the crumb : then put the oysters into a stew-pan, with their liquor, and the crumbs that came out of the rolls, and a good lump of butter ; stew them together five or six minutes : then put in a spoonful of good cream ; fill the skeleton rolls with the compound, and lay the bit of crust carefully on the top again, setting them in the oven to crisp. Three form a side dish.

13. *Oyster Omelet.*—Having strained the liquor from three

dozen plump native oysters, mince them small ; omitting the hard part, or gristle. If you cannot get large oysters, you should have forty or fifty small ones. Break into a shallow pan six, seven, or eight eggs, according to the quantity of minced oysters. Omit half the whites, and (having beaten the eggs till very light, thick, and smooth,) mix the oysters gradually into them, adding a little cayenne pepper, and some powdered nutmeg. Put three ounces or more of the best fresh butter into a small frying-pan, if you have no pan especially for omelets. Place it over a clear fire, and when the butter (which should be previously cut up) has come to a boil, put in the omelet-mixture ; stir it till it begins to set ; and fry it a light brown, lifting the edge several times by slipping a knife under it, and taking care not to cook it too much or it will shrivel and become tough. When done, clap a large hot plate or dish on the top of the omelet, and turn it quickly and carefully out of the pan. Fold it over, and serve it up immediately. This quantity will make one large or two small omelets. The omelet pan should be smaller than a common frying-pan, and lined with tin. In a large pan the omelet will spread too much, and become thin like a pancake. Never turn an omelet while frying, as that will make it heavy and tough. When done, brown it by holding a red-hot salamander close above the top.

Having given a baker's dozen of the most approved receipts for dressing oysters, I have only to add that the oyster, as an accessory, enters into many dishes, particularly into fricassees, is served with sweetbreads, fowl, and veal, and, as we all know from "Tom and Jerry," "gentlemen" eat oysters as sauce to rump steak ; which, by the way, I, for one, regard as the ruin of both oyster and steak. I cannot refrain from adding the following, both little known in this country, yet both equally good:—

14. *Cabbage with Oysters and Fried Larks.*—When the cab-

bage has been cooked with a little Rhenish wine, Chablis, or Champagne, some good butter is melted, in which the oysters are put with their beards and liquor, and having been fried a little with the butter, they are put with the cabbage and and cooked again together, and then served up with the larks.

15.—*Fried Hind Legs of Frogs with Oysters.*—The hind legs of frogs are fried in the usual manner; when they are nearly done, some oysters with Parmesan cheese and a little pepper are added to them, and when done they are served up. This dish is undeniable, and is as much relished abroad as whitebait with us.

In closing this chapter, let me remind all cooks that the success in preparing the above-mentioned dishes depends on the goodness and freshness of the oysters used for this purpose. Very erroneous is the opinion that oysters which are not fresh are yet good enough to be fried and to be used for sauces. The greatest delicacy is a fresh oyster, but a stale one is a source of the greatest disgust, and only fit to regale the ghost of that Royal George who, when living, never relished a raw oyster unless the shell was self-opened on the dish.

CHAPTER VIII.

THE OYSTER AND THE DOCTOR.

Oyster-eating in Prussia ; Disgusting Wagers ; Oysters better
than Pills ; A Universal Remedy ; Professional Opinions ;
When Ladies should eat them ; Repugnance overcome ;
Oysters as an external application ; Chemical Analysis ;
How to tell if dead before opening.

WHEN in Prussia, I once asked a person who did a
large retail business in oysters, what class of
persons he found to be his best customers, and what
was the number of oysters daily consumed by each individual?

" The morning scarcely begins to dawn," he replied,
" ere ladies and gentlemen, boys and girls, and servants,
both male and female, make their appearance, not only
from my immediate neighbourhood, but also from the most
remote parts of the city, when, on an average, every one
buys from half a dozen up to a dozen, in addition to
their purchases for the several families, and in accordance with their requirements."

And those who do likewise in Great Britain and Ireland will soon find out the benefit of this nutritive food
taken thus early on an empty stomach. I once heard of
an individual who made a bet that he would eat twelve
dozen oysters, washed down by twelve glasses of Champagne, while the cathedral clock of the city which he in-
habited was striking twelve. He won his bet by placing a

dozen fresh oysters in twelve wine glasses, and having swallowed the oysters, he washed down each dozen with a glass of Champagne. I should not have mentioned this disgusting feat, but to add that he felt no evil effects from the oysters, proving incontestably the digestive and sanitary properties of this mollusk.

There is a similar tale showing equally the effects of oysters on the human digestion. Four persons met one Saturday night at an hotel, and made the following bet: each person was to call for whatever he might fancy, either to eat or to drink, and he who kept longest awake was to have no share in the liquidation of the bill. This settled, one of the party made a private arrangement with one of the waiters, promising him a reward if, in case of his evincing the slightest drowsiness, he would bring him forthwith twenty-five oysters.

This was accordingly done; but the waiters had to be constantly relieved until 11 o'clock on the following Monday morning, when, observing his three companions quietly asleep, our oyster-eating friend called for the landlord, and declared himself triumphantly the winner, attributing his good fortune entirely to the oyster.

Wise people eat oysters and eschew pills; take lumps of delight, instead of lumps of nausea; uphold the Sweetings, Pims, and Lynns, and have nothing to do with the Holloways, Morisons, and "Old Parrs."

When suffering from almost incurable indigestion, by taking oysters daily, they very soon find the most agreeable effects on the human kitchen and laboratory; its functions become regular, without the use of strong medicines, always dangerous. Depression of spirits and other disagreeable feelings consequent on impaired digestion soon cease to affect them; they become cheerful and happy, and are enabled again to see clearly through the misty atmosphere which has hitherto enclosed them in a kind of living shroud; physical powers return, headaches disappear, and the heretofore dyspeptic, sour, unhappy tempered man becomes a pleasant and joyous companion, full of life himself, and inspiriting to those around him.

I have lived a good deal abroad, and am induced to ascribe much of the vivacity of the French to their intense love of oysters. During a long residence in France, I never met with a Frenchman or Frenchwoman who said nay to a dish of good fresh oysters; in fact, they have a craving for the " breedy creatures," which in many persons almosts amounts to gluttony, and then, and then only, does this craving lead to mischief.

Physicians of old recommended the oyster as a general remedy, and employed it on all occasions with success. It has been proved beyond dispute that it possesses a remarkable vivifying influence in all cases where the nervous organs are affected, more than any other food. Oysters taken before mid-day with a glass of wine produce a most salutary effect. The nerves and muscles regain their strength, and the body its mental and physical powers, bringing cheerfulness and energy to compete with the duties of the day. If not a cure, at all events, an oyster diet, under medical supervision, brings unquestionable relief to those who are suffering from pulmonary complaints, indigestion, or nervous affections.

Dr. Leroy was in the habit of swallowing, every

morning before breakfast, two dozen oysters, and used always to say to his friends, presenting them with the shells: "There, behold the fountain of my youthful strength !"

Percy relates having seen a large number of wounded persons, exhausted by the loss of blood and bad treatment, who were entirely kept up by eating oysters; and Dr. Lenac considered them the most nourishing food in existence.

Oysters are strongly recommended to all persons suffering from weak digestion ; and Dr. Pasquier adds, that "they may be given with great advantage to persons of intemperate habits, who, by inefficacious medical treatment have fallen into debility and lowness of spirits." He also recommends oysters to all who are suffering from the gout. I myself knew a person last winter, who was suffering from influenza, which, from his being an aged man, threatened the most serious consequences, who was entirely cured by eating oysters.

Oysters increase the blood without heating the system, and hence when a wound has caused much loss of blood, the eating of oysters not only prevents fever, but replaces the loss which no other remedy can effect. The great Boerhaave affirms to have known a tall, strong man, who had fallen into a decline, and who, after all other remedies had proved useless, by the use of oysters rapidly recovered, became strong, and died ninety-three years old.

But to ladies, particularly, do I recommend oysters as the best of all light meals between breakfast and dinner. At the period of a lady's married life, when nausea is prevalent, a few fresh oysters, taken raw in their own liquor, with no addition but a little pepper, and a fairy slice of French roll or other light bread, stops the feeling of sickness, and keeps up the stamina unimpaired. During the time, too, when a young child most requires maternal care and attention, the mother's diet of oysters will impart strength to the infant, and tend much to alleviate the pains of its first teething.

I am well aware that some persons have a repugnance to the eating of oysters, and that it may be difficult to overcome the dislike. However, as a proof that oysters in general are nice to the taste, let me mention that children under two years of age eat them with great appetite; and it is only after having discontinued eating any for some time that they take a dislike to them.

I have often had the opportunity of overcoming this dislike, and the result was always satisfactory. The method is very simple. Take a French roll (or a piece of milk-bread) thinly buttered, and put on it the oyster deprived of its beard, squeezing a few drops of lemon and peppering it. "Well, after all, the taste of the oyster is really fine!" is the usual exclamation, and after that the person has eaten them in their natural state with gusto.

When eaten for health, an oyster is best swallowed in its own liquor the moment the shell is opened; or if too cold for the stomach, a sprinkling of pepper will remedy the evil. Vinegar counteracts the effect of the oyster enriching the blood; so when the oyster is eaten medicinally it must be excluded. Dr. Evans, in No. 834 of the "Family Herald" says, that when too many oysters or other shell-fish has been taken, the unpleasant sensation excited by such excess may be removed by drinking half a pint of hot milk. Persons of delicate constitutions will do well always to take hot milk after oysters.

But the oyster was also formerly used externally as a remedy no less than taken internally for its medicinal properties. Its very abundance is a clear proof of the bounty and goodness of Providence, furnishing us, at one and the same time, with such delicious food, and so universal a remedy for the ills which man is heir to. Ambrois Paré, physician to Charles IX., and the only Protestant whom the king sought to save from the terrible massacre of St. Bartholomew, by shutting him up in his own closet, recommends oysters smashed in their shells as an excellent poultice. "This animal, so used," says he, "diminishes pain, and removes all heat and inflammation in a remarkable manner." As the opinion of one, of whom the king himself declared that "a man so useful to all the world ought not to perish like a dog," it may be admitted to a place in my little book, more particularly as it is borne out by Paul Egona, who also recommends oysters being smashed and saturated with their own liquor as the very best of all poultices for sores or boils.

Let me, as a close to this chapter, add a few words on the chemical analysis of the oyster. The animal itself contains a great proportion of phosphate of iron and lime, a considerable quantity of osmozone, and a certain amount of gluten and isinglass, being of a peculiar nature, which phosphorus penetrates like an element.

F

It also contains a great quantity of particles of salt, the same as that of the sea-water in which it lives.

The oyster-liquor, or, as I have said, more properly speaking, its life's blood, contains a great amount of hydroidum, kali, sulphur of lime, sulphur of magnesia, some organic matter, osmazone, and a very little salt. The shell is composed of a very intimate mixture of salt, carbonic lime, and animal mucus. It exhibits, also, phosphate of lime and magnesia in small quantities, as also sulphuretted hydrogen.

At the moment in which natural death ensues, all animal matter begins to show its chemical affinities by separating again into the elements of which it consists; and as at such times it is always more or less of a poisonous nature, it is well to study the method by which it may be known whether an oyster was living or dead when its shell is opened. This can be seen at a glance. If the muscle appears sunk, it is a proof that the animal was living; but if it appears higher and above the oyster, it was dead before it was opened, and the animal is, consequently, unwholesome and unfit for food.

CHAPTER IX.

THE OYSTER ABROAD.

British Oysters in Ostend Quarters ; the Whitstable in a Slow Coach ; Holstein, Schleswig, and Heligoland Natives ; Norwegian and Bremer Oysters ; American Oysters ; French Oysters ; Dutch Oysters ; Mediterranean Oysters, and Classical Judges.

I AM not writing a book for the man of science. I could not if I would. It is for those who love oysters for the eating that I have turned author; and all the facts which are strung together in the last chapters were put there for their delectation, and not for the sake of raising the smile which I saw just now pass over the face of my friend Sawbones when I mentioned oyster-poultices. Just because I am not scientific, but only practical, I shall not trouble myself to notice any of the many species of oysters, both at home and abroad, which, though pretty in themselves, never find their way to the table, which is the sole field of my discoveries.

I shall therefore begin my list of foreign oysters with the best of them all, the next of kin to our Native, and next to it the best oyster in the world.

1. *The Ostend Oyster* is nothing more than the real British oyster, cleaned and fattened in the Ostend oyster-beds. It has a fine, thin, transparent but deep shell, the upper shell being quite flat; it is very full,

white, and fat, has a very small beard, and is very digestible. During a south-west wind, which brings to these beds the microscopic spores of sea vegetation and animalcules upon which it delights to feed, from the channel, its beard is of a green colour. The Ostend oyster is much prized in Berlin, which it reaches the quickest of any from the sea, (in thirty-six to forty hours,) and consequently lives there several days, remains the longest fresh, and can be sent farthest. Last winter Ostend oysters were sent to Moscow and Odessa, where they arrived still good and tasty. The former were seventeen days, and the latter eleven days on their way. Scarcely any other kind of oysters could be sent to such a distance. In the autumn of 1847, after the opening of the Cologne-Minden Railway, the first trial was made of sending these oysters to Berlin, *via* Cologne. The result was most satisfactory; they sold for $1\frac{1}{2}$ thalers the hundred. This caused no little sensation, especially among the old oyster dealers, who were accustomed to receive from five to six, even from eight to nine thalers per hundred. The good folks of Berlin are now supplied with abundant fresh and fine oysters. The Ostend natives may be obtained from the owner of the oyster beds in Ostend. I speak of Berlin, as the Germans are great oyster-eaters, and the North, in a great measure, is supplied from thence.

In Brussels, Antwerp, Ghent, Bruges, and Lille, Ostend oysters are eaten with slices of home-baked bread, and butter. They are served up in their shells, open, and not broken apart. They have a tender, fragrant, and melting flesh, and are only half the size of ordinary oysters; but they gain in thickness what they lose in size. In Flanders and the Netherlands they are known under the name of " English oysters," but are called in Paris after the name of the beds where they are reared. They are in reality Edinburgh " Natives," cleaned and fattened in the Ostend oyster-beds, and hence called Belgian or Ostend oysters.

The oyster of Ostend cannot be too much recommended to gourmets. It is to the common oyster what a chicken is to an old hen. It is a draught of bitter ale to a thirsty palate. It is a known fact, that after having abstained from food for a long time, the first oyster one eats produces a kind of unusual rictus (or opening of the mouth), the reason of which physiologists have never been able to explain. This same sensation is produced in eating an Ostend oyster, but it is much sweeter, more lasting, and much more delightful. If the Romans had ever known them they would have sung their praises both in verse and prose, and would by far have preferred them to their sadly over-praised oysters from the Lucrine Sea.

The only oysters which can be brought into competition with those of Ostend in the same markets are the Whitstable oysters, which have only recently become an article of trade on the Continent. These are also " natives" from the Channel, generally larger than the former, but unequal, not being sorted, very fat and full, but much more tender, and do not keep fresh so long. The cause of this may be that they are first taken from Whitstable to London, where they are packed up and sent by sea and rail to Hamburgh and Berlin, which takes always from six to seven days. They have a fine flavour, and are by some people preferred to the Ostend oysters : although the latter, generally speaking, occupy the first rank. These two species, and that of Holstein, are the best oysters to be met with in the north of Europe.

2. *Channel Oysters.*—The oysters which, more particularly in the north of Germany, are an article of trade, come from the Bay of St. Brieux and the Rock of Cancale, on the British Channel, between the castle of that name, Mount St. Michael, and St. Malo, and from the Channel between Calais and its extreme point near Falmouth. The bottom of this sea is flat and firm, and its stream near the bottom not very strong, both favourable circumstances for the propagation of oysters. This propagation must be very considerable, and the banks where the oysters breed very extensive, since, in spite of the continual dredging, they produce a sufficient quantity without any apparent decrease, to guard against which, the new beds of St. Brieux, mentioned in the first chapter, are carefully supplied. The dredging lasts generally from the middle of September till the end of May; during the other months the fishing should properly be discontinued, because the spawning, which then takes place, would be disturbed, and because during that time the oyster is generally not fit for food.

3. *Holstein Oysters* are very good and fine, but the sea-banks do not afford enough for the present consumption, so that it is necessary to have good connexions in order to obtain real and good Holstein oysters. They are easily distinguished from all the other oysters by their size, the thin, greenish-blue shells, especially the

lower shell. The upper shell is always concave, by which they are the more easily distinguished from the Heligolanders, which have always a strong convex upper shell. As to the little animal itself, it is very fat, white, thick, and tender, and therefore very digestible. It has only a small beard, by which it is distinguished from the Norwegian and Scottish oyster, which, by the appearance of the shell, might be mistaken for the Holstein oyster by novices in gastronomy. These delicate favourites are to be obtained from the lessees of the Royal Oyster-banks on the western coast of Holstein in Flensburg, in the kingdom of Denmark.

4. *The Schleswick Oyster of Husum and Silt* is very like the former—almost undistinguishable. It is very excellent, but seldom exported, and consumed for the most part in Kiel. The two last-named oysters are often taken to St. Petersburg by sailors, when making the passage to and fro.

5. *The Heligolanders* are very large; have thick shells, which renders the duty and carriage very high, but are not at all fine, and generally sold in all the innocence of ignorance by dealers as Holstein oysters.

Have nothing to do with *Norwegian oysters;* I only mention them here as things to be shunned. *Bremer oysters,* the *Neuwerkers,* and the *Wangerogers,* however, deserve a better fate.

6. *The Oyster of the Bay of Biscay* is of the same size as that of Holstein, with a very large beard, like those caught in the south of England. The beard, like the oyster itself, is quite grass green—a quality which is to be found generally only with oysters from Dieppe, Cancale, and the Marennes. Its flavour is very fine and

good, but great care must be taken, in opening the shell and detaching the oyster, not to break the double shell, which they mostly possess, for this contains sulphuretted hydrogen, which gives a bad smell and flavour to the oyster, and poisons the stomach of the consumer.

7. *American Oysters*, though, to my taste, by no means so delicate as others I have mentioned, are nevertheless superior for cooking. For my own part, although I have stated that pepper, vinegar, lemon juice, and other stimulating ingredients, are commonly made use of when eating the oyster, I offer, in all courtesy, the decided opinion, that the taste must be vitiated that can swallow such in preference to the delicate, fresh, luscious, charming little morsel, saturated merely, or perhaps the word ought to be merely bedewed, like the rose on a summer morning, by its own liquid life's blood. Americans, themselves, generally prefer their large oysters even to our British Natives.

8. *French Oysters.*—The French oysters are chiefly taken from beds in the Bays of Cancale and St. Brieux, from Marennes, from Havre and Dieppe, from Dunkirk, and from the Bay of Biscay. The three first are very fine, but the distance to Paris is too great; they are therefore dear in that capital. Those from Dunkirk are similar to those of Ostend, but not quite so fine; and those from the Bay of Biscay are quite green, and highly esteemed in the south of France, especially at Bordeaux.

9. *Dutch Oysters* are both good and dear. The four sorts I recommend are Seelanders, Vliessingers, Middleburgers, and Vieringers. The latter are almost the finest and best, but uncommonly dear, and are mostly consumed in Holland.

10. *Mediterranean Oysters.*—I have already referred
to classical authorities for the character the ancients
gave those of Circe and the Lucrine Sea ; and the old
rule, " *de mortius nil,*" forbids me to say in what rank
I place Horace the inimitable, Seneca the wise, and
Pliny the naturalist, as judges of what an oyster should
be. Where ignorance is bliss, people can be very happy.
Till the Turk, by an accidental fire, had become ac-
quainted with the taste of roast pork, there were many
less fires in Stamboul than now. Till the Romans found
the Rutupians, the Lucrine flourished ; so did Circe.

CHAPTER X.

OF all beautiful things in the world the pearl is the
rarest and most beautiful. Nothing can exceed it,
nothing can equal it, although they try very hard in
"French" and "Roman" ways, in glassy globules
which continually crack, or in round spots of wax,
which, instead of adorning, adhere to the neck of
beauty, and when old age comes upon it, turn yellow
and wrinkled like the skin of a dowager. Nay, nothing
can well imitate it, although art has gone somewhat
near it. But to a knowing eye one might as well seek
to imitate truth, or palm away upon the unwary a copy
of true virgin innocence as to imitate a pearl. We
know all the answers that the dowagers can make; we
know that the imitations are "so cheap," so pretty;
we know that certain dowagers—witness Margaret,
Duchess Dowager of Lancaster—sell their real pearls
and wear cunning imitations; we know that they in
vain try to persuade themselves that the false are as

good as the true ones; but only look hard at the orna-
ments, and the duchess is abashed. To test false pearls,
one has only to put a true one by them, and the "difference," as advertisers say, "will be at once perceived."

Let us devote this last portion of our book to the history of the pearl. Its very names are pretty. *Looloo,*
Mootoo, Mootie, Margaritæ, Perles, Perlii, Perlas, Pearls,
all sweet, pretty, mouth-rounding names, but worthy
to be applied to the lustrous and beautiful spheres
which we call pearls. *Principium culmenque omnium*
rerum pretii tenent: " Of all things, pearls," said
Pliny, two thousand years ago, " kept the very top,
highest, best, and first price." What was true then
is true now. There are few things so immortal as
good taste. Let us pay something " on account "
of our debt to the oyster. Having regarded that
placid creditor as an article of food, I now propose
to treat him as an assistant to the toilet. And, looking
at him in that point of view, here is not a bad instal-
ment of the aforesaid debt, contributed by Barry Cornwall.

> " Within the midnight of her hair,
>   Half-hidden in its deepest deeps,
> A single peerless, priceless pearl
>   (All filmy-eyed) for ever sleeps.
> Without the diamond's sparkling eyes,
> The ruby's blushes—there it lies,
> Modest as the tender dawn,
> When her purple veil's withdrawn—
> The flower of gems, a lily cold and pale.
> Yet, what doth all avail?—

All its beauty, all its grace?
All the honours of its place?
He who pluck'd it from its bed,
In the far blue Indian Ocean,
Lieth, without life or motion,
In his earthy dwelling—dead!
All his children, one by one,
When they look up to the sun,
Curse the toil by which he drew
The treasure from its bed of blue."

Costly as pearls are, they are merely the calcareous production of Mollusks. Diamonds have elsewhere been shown to be merely charcoal; the pearl is little else but concentric layers of membrane and carbonate of lime. All Mollusks are instances of that beneficent law of nature, that the hard parts accommodate themselves to the soft. The common naked snail, the mussel, cockle, oyster, garden helix, strombus, and nautilus, elegant or rough, rare or common, each illustrate this grand law. The body of a soft consistence is enclosed in an elastic skin. From this skin calcareous matter is continually exuded. This protects the animal, and forms the shell. Where the waves are rough, and rocks superabundant, then the shell is rough, hard, stony, fit to weather anything; where only smooth water and halcyon days are to be looked for, Nature, which never works in vain, provides but paper sides and an egg-shell boat, such as the little nautilus navigates and tacks and steers in.

Besides forming the rough outside, the calcareous exuvium, the mucus of the oyster, and other mollusks, form that beautiful substance, so smooth and polished, and dyed with rainbow tints and a glorious opalescence, which, be it as common as luxury has made it, still charms the eye. This is the lining of the shell, the mother-of-pearl, nacre. "The inside of the shell," said old Dampier—that old sailor with a poet's mind— "is more glorious even than the pearl itself."

It is glorious; it has the look of the morning, and the tint of the evening sky; the colours of the prism chastened, softened, retained, and made perpetual in it: this is mother-o'-pearl.

To render its bed always soft and cosy, to lie warm, packed as one might at Malvern in wet sheets, seems to be the oyster's pleasure. This singular exuvium, this mucus, not only creates pleasure, but alleviates pain. Some irritating substance, some internal worry and annoyance, it may be a dead embryo, or a grain of sand insinuates itself, and, lo! the creature covers it with this substance to ease off its unkind tooth, and converts it into a pearl.

That is the way they are made, these wondrous gems! And very beautiful is the thought that the most highly prized of gems should be but the effect of a creature to ease off a sorrow. Every one knows Shakspeare's wondrously fine reflection upon the uses of sorrow and adversity, which,

> " Like the toad, ugly and venomous,
> Bears yet a precious jewel in its head."

The precious jewel of the toad, which some critics and commentators have endeavoured to prove its glittering eye, has long been exploded. Our old alchemists believed in the toadstone; we do not. The fable remains in its pristine beauty; but here is one truth equally beautiful, that the adversity of the oyster turns to a jewel so costly and glorious, that monarchs reckon it amongst the records of their houses and conquered provinces. May we ever turn our sorrows and troubles to as good an account; may we ever continue to do so, for assuredly some men do. The best of men are those who are tried by affliction and trouble, or those who have some deep and secret care, which they hide in their hearts, and which makes them wiser and better. Shelley has a theory that poets are made somewhat after the fashion of pearls, or that, at any rate, their poetry is so produced. He sings—

> "Most wretched men
> Are cradled into poetry by wrong;
> They learn in suffering, what they teach in song."

We have very little doubt but that the true poetry from which the world learns anything worth learning is so produced.

There have been other theories as to the production of the pearl, some holding that the interior formation which we state to be a grain of sand, is a dead ovum which the fish attempts to exude. This theory, too, has its supporters.

"If," said Sir Everard Home, "if I can prove that this, the richest jewel in a monarch's crown, which cannot be imitated by any art of man" (he is rather wrong there; it can be imitated, and wonderfully imitated too,) "either in beauty of form or brilliancy of lustre, is the abortive egg of an oyster enveloped in its own nacre, who will not be struck with wonder and astonishment?" Wonder and astonishment are words which scarcely exist now. Science has shown so many wonders that we are hardly astonished at anything; but Sir Everard's assertion admits of proof. A pearl cut in two exhibits the concentric layers like an onion, as may be seen through a strong lens; and in the centre is a round hole, very minute it may be, but wherein the ovum has been deposited.

Sometimes the ovum, or sand, or enclosed substance has attached itself to the shell, and has then been covered with mucus, forming a pearl which cannot be separated from the shell. There are several specimens of such pearls in the British Museum.

The great beauty in pearls is their opalescence, and a lustre which, as we have before observed, however clever the imitation, has never yet been given to artificial pearls. Sir Everard Home supposes that this lustre arises from the highly polished coat of the centre shell, the pearl itself being diaphanous. Sir David Brewster accounts for it by the pearl and mother-of-pearl having a grooved substance on its surface resembling the minute corrugations often seen on substances covered with oil, paint, or varnish. Philosophers are sometimes not very explanatory. Sir David means to say that beneath the immediate polish of the pearl there are certain wavelets and dimples from which the light is reflected. "The direction of the grooves," again to quote Sir David, "is in every case at right angles to the line joining the coloured image; hence, in irregularly formed mother-of-pearl, where the grooves are often circular, and have every possible direction, the coloured images appear irregularly scattered round the ordinary image."

In the regular pearl these are crowded, from its spherical form, into a small space; hence its marvellous appearance of white unformed light, and hence its beauty and value.

To prove the translucency of the pearl, we have only to hold one which is split to a candle, where, by interposing coloured substance or light, we shall have the colour transmitted through the pearl. Curious as is the formation of the pearl, we have yet a cognate substance to it. What we call *bezoar*, and the Hindoos *faduj*, is a concretion of a deepish olive-green colour found in the stomach of goats, dogs, cows, or other animals: the hog bezoar, the bovine bezoar, and the camel bezoar; this last the Hindoos turn into a yellow paint; but the harder substances the Hindoo jewellers polish and thread and use as jewels; so that from the stomach of the lower animals, and from the secretions of a shell-fish, the still grasping, prying, worrying, proud, vain-glorious, busy man gets him an ornament for her whom he most loves, for him whom he most honours.

The question of obtaining pearls and of slaying divers, of feeding sharks with human limbs, of the eyeballs starting and the tympanum of the ear bursting, of the pains, perils, and penalties of the pearl divers, must be touched incidentally in any true account of this precious gem.

Vanity demands the aid of Cruelty, and for her gratification human sacrifices are still made.

In the Persian Gulf, at Ceylon, and in the Red Sea, the early sources of the Greeks and Romans, we yet find our supply. Pearls are also found in the Indian Ocean along the Coromandel coast and elsewhere; as also in the Gulf of California; but the two grand headquarters are in Bahrein Island, in the Persian Gulf, and in the Bay of Condalchy, in the Gulf of Manaar, off the Island of Ceylon.

The fishery at Ceylon is a monopoly of the British Government, but, like many Government monopolies, it is said to cost a great deal more than it produces. In 1804 Government leased it for £120,000 per annum; in 1828 it only yielded £28,000.* It is a desert and barren spot; no one can fall in love with it; sands and coral reefs are not picturesque; yet, in its season, it attracts more to its shores than one of our best watering-places. Divers, merchants, Arab-hawkers, drillers, jewellers, and talkers; fish-sellers, butchers, boat-caulkers, and Hindoo Robinsons and Walkers are all found there. The period is limited to six weeks, or two months at most, from February to April; and whilst they are making money these people are rather eager, look you. But the fishers themselves, victims of cruelty as they are, are also victims to their own super-

---

* The pearl fishery at Ceylon, however, has been very profitable during the present year, the yield being sometimes worth from 10,000 dollars to 30,000 dollars per day. An attempt is being made to re-establish the pearl fishery in the Gulf of California. Some very fine pearls were found there nearly a century ago.

stition and ignorance. A Hindoo or Parsee blesses the
water to drive away the sharks; a diver may be fright-
ened or ill, and the holidays are so numerous, that the
actual work-days amount only to thirty in the season.

The boats assembled sail at ten at night, a signal gun
being then let off. They then set sail, reach the banks
before daybreak, and at sunrise the divers begin to take
their "headers." They continue at this work till noon,
when a breeze starting up, they return. The cargoes
are taken out before the night sets in, and the divers
are refreshed.

Each boat carries twenty men—ten rowers and ten
divers—besides a chief, or pilot. The divers work five
at a time alternately, leaving the others time to recruit.
To go down quickly they use a large stone of red
granite, which they catch hold of with their foot.
Each diver holds a net-work bag in his right hand,
closes his nostrils with his left, or with a piece of bent
horn, and descends to the bottom. There he darts
about him as quickly as he can, picking up with toes
and fingers, and putting the oysters into his net-work
bag. When this is full, or he is exhausted, he pulls the
rope, and is drawn, leaving the stone to be pulled up
after him. When the oysters are very plentiful, the
diver may bring up one hundred and fifty at a dip.

After this violent exertion, blood flows from nose,
ears, and eyes. The divers cannot exceed generally one
minute's immersion. One and a half, and even two,
have been reached by extraordinary efforts. Those who
can endure four and five minutes are spoken of. One
also we are told of—an apocryphal fellow, we should

think—who coming in 1797 from Arjango, stayed under water six minutes.

The divers live not to a great age. Heart diseases, surfeits, sores, blood-shot eyes, staggering limbs, and bent backs—these are part of their wages. Sometimes they die on reaching the surface, suddenly, as if struck by a shot.

At Bahrein, the annual amount produced by the pearl fishery may be reckoned at from £200,000 to £240,000; add to this purchases made by the merchants of Abootabee, and we have £360,000 to include the whole pearl trade of the Gulf, since, through their agents at Bahrein, merchants from Constantinople, Bagdad, Alexandria, Timbuctoo, New York, Calcutta, Paris, St. Petersburg, Holy Moscowa, or London, make their purchases.

"But," says our credible informant, "I have not put down the sum at *one-sixth* of that told me by the native merchants." But even then an enormous amount is that, to be used in mere ornament, and in one article only.

Well, not exactly ornament. "In Eastern lands," says Mr. Thomas Moore, "they talk in flowers." Very flowery certainly is their talk. They also, good easy people, take pearls for physic—not for dentifrice—Easterns always having white teeth, apparently, so far as I have been able to judge, without the trouble of cleaning them —but as a regular dose. They call it *majoon;* it is an electuary, and myriads of small seed pearls are ground to impalpable powder to make it. As for the adulteration in this article, doubtless to be found, I say nothing. The simple lime from the inside of the shell would be

just as white and just as good. Common magnesia
would have the same effect; but, good sirs, if an old
Emir, or rich Bonze, wishes to pay an enormous price
for something to swallow to comfort his good old inside,
why not? Do not let us brag too much : from the
time of old Gower, doctor of physic, to Dr. Cheyne,
we have, sir, swallowed everything, from toads' brains
to the filings of a murderer's irons, as very proper
physic.

The Bahrein fishery-boats amount to 1500, and the
trade is in the hands of merchants who possess much
capital. This they lend out at cent. per cent.; they buy
up, and they beat down; they juggle, cheat, rig the
market, rob in a legal way a whole boat's crew, grow
enormously rich, and preach morality.

Nor do they forget superstition. In the chief boat,
when they fish, sits a jolly old cheat, a magician, called
the binder of sharks, who waves about his skinny hands,
jumps, howls, incants, and otherwise exerts his cabalistic
powers, and will not allow the divers, nor are they
willing, to descend till he declares the moment pro-
pitious. To add some weight to their devotions, they
debar themselves of food or drink during this *Mumbo-
Jumbo* play, but afterwards a species of toddy makes
them like " Roger the Monk,"—" excessively drunk."

The true shape of the pearl should be a perfect sphere.
In India, and elsewhere, those of the largest size find
the readiest sale, and realize immense prices. The very
finest pearls are sent to Europe, and of these the very
finest of the fine are sent to London and Paris. Thence
the great people of the land procure their choice speci-

mens. The late Emperor of Russia used to purchase for his wife—of whom he was exceedingly fond, and who has lately joined him in that bourne from which neither traveller, emperor, king, nor beggar ever returns— the very finest pearl he could procure : a virgin pearl and a perfect sphere was what he sought, for he would not have any that had been worn by others. After five-and-twenty years' search, he presented to the Empress such a necklace as had never been seen before.

Immense prices have been given and are still given for pearls. Julius Cæsar, in love with the mother of Marcus Brutus, is said to have presented her with a pearl worth £48,417 10s., which we can believe or not, according to our natures. Cleopatra, as all the world has read, drank, dissolved in vinegar, a pearl which cost £80,729 of our money, and, as we know from Shakspeare, Marc Antony sent to her " a treasure of an oyster" of wondrous beauty. Clodius, the glutton (surely a gourmet, not a gourmand), swallowed one worth £8072 18s. One of the modern pearls was bought by Tavernier at Catifa, and sold by him to the Shah of Persia for £110,000; another was obtained by Philip II. of Spain, off the Columbian coast, which weighed 250 carats, and was valued at 14,400 ducats, which is equal to about £13,996.

Pliny, the naturalist, tells us of a pearl which was valued at £80,000 sterling. That which Philip II. had was nearly as large as a pigeon's egg. Pliny's was somewhat smaller. But size is not alone the test of value. Shape and form must be taken into considera-tion. Some pearls are very curiously misshapen, and of

so large a size that it would seem a wonder how the fish
could exist with them in the shell. These misshapen
pearls are generally of an uneven surface and lustre, and
are prized by the Eastern jewellers very much, and
were also sought after by the fanciful goldsmiths and
enamellers of the *cinque-cento* period, when they were set
into sword-hilts, or formed into toys or gems, just as
the fancy and shape might suggest. We have seen one
large long pearl mounted by a Spanish jeweller into the
order of the golden fleece, the legs and head of the sheep
being of gold, the body formed by the pearl. Amongst
the loot taken at Lucknow was a set of miniature animals and birds, all formed of large but misshapen pearls,
the tails, heads, eyes, &c., of the creatures being of gold
set with diamonds. Any one who has seen much me-
diæval work in the precious metals, or the illuminated
pages of early printed books on vellum, of Italian exe-
cution, will be able to recall many curious instances of
this quaint kind of *vertu*.

The largest pearl of which we have heard was one
spoken of by Böethius, the size of a muscadine pear. It
was named the *Incomparable*, and weighed thirty carats
or five pennyweights. Tavernier's pearl would, if en-
graved, well illustrate the rocky, eccentric, and oft-
times triangular shapes in which these gems are found.
They often adhere to the shell, and cannot be removed
without the saw. After such an operation they would
merely rank as half pearls, which, by the way, are
those generally mounted in jewellery and rings.

Did our scope allow of a description of the manufac-
ture from fish scales of the substitute for the real pearl,

the marvellously clever imitation which is worn, wittingly, by many a gracious lady, and unwittingly by many another, we should have another interesting story to tell. But these imitations may be considered as frauds upon our placid creditor the oyster—or, shall we say, compositions with him, and beneath the notice of, debtors who are trying to behave honestly to a bivalve.

Properly speaking, however, the Pearl oyster (*Avicula margaritacea*), from which the greater number of pearls, and the largest quantity of mother-of-pearl is obtained, is not an oyster strictly so called, but belongs to an allied genus. The pearl oyster is an oval-pointed recurved-edged mussel; the lower shell with a hood-shaped hollow point, the upper one like a cover, leafy and pearly, of a rosy purple-white colour. The common oyster (*Ostrea edulis*), on the contrary, has a round-oval mussel-shell, thin towards the edges, with tiled leaves adhering to one another, the upper shell quite flat. Some variety exists in these, some having elongated edges, owing to the difference of age.

Gentle reader! when Queen Mary, whom men call "Bloody Mary," died, and Queen Elizabeth, Protestant Elizabeth, came to the throne, Osorius, the good Bishop of Arcoburge, a staunch bishop of the Church of Rome, sent her a sugared pill, which he hoped would at once convert the queen, and drive out the "obnoxious heresy" from the land. That all might read it, he himself wrote it in Latin: "*Epistola ad Clarissimam Principam Elizabetham;*" had it translated into French, which honest old Strype says "gave great offence," as "*une bien longue*

et docte Epistre à Madame Elizabeth, Royne d'Angleterre;"
and to gild the nasty thing, called it, in English, "A
Perle for a Prince;" but all the ingenuity of quackery
could not disguise the drastic pill, and neither the queen
nor her lieges would swallow it. I have seen all three
books in the Grenville Library in the British Museum,
and at once pronounce them nothing but "mock" pearls..
Now, I have extracted for your delectation a real pearl
out of the Oyster, in the shape of this little book. It is
Christmas-tide. Cherish it for those best of pearls,
kindly thoughts and loving remembrances, which the
Oyster calls into being when the Holly and the Mistle-
toe deck our walls.

LONDON : WILLIAM STEVENS, PRINTER, BELL YARD, TEMPLE BAR.

www.ingramcontent.com/pod-product-compliance
Lightning Source LLC
Chambersburg PA
CBHW021412090426
42742CB00009B/1116